Find the Flipping Deals

The Money-Making Strategies Successful
Real Estate Investors Don't Want You to
Know

By Jason Lucchesi

Find the Flipping Deals

ISBN-13: 978-1985408166

ISBN-10: 1985408163

Cover design by Sooraj Mathew
Edited by Hilary Jastram

Dedication

For my children Brady, Gavin, and Cordelia. Be amazing every single day. You can be and do anything you want in this life.

For my wife, Jamie. Thank you for holding down the fort and being such a rock for our family. You're the glue that keeps us all together.

Also, to all of our service members and vets, who have fought to protect this great country, the United States of America. Thank you for your service and the sacrifices you've made.

Table of Contents

Introduction

This book was created with the intention of giving investors at any level the information they need to succeed and operate a thriving real estate business. When I first got started back in 2008, I was pulled in this direction and that direction. I couldn't figure out how to start, where to find deals, and even how to close deals. I watched house flipping shows and was misled all over the place. It was an awful feeling, so I decided to create this book, so other individuals, real estate investors, entrepreneurs, and anyone else who desired to get into real estate would not have the same trial and error period that I'd had. At that time, I was stuck. When I began my career as a real estate investor, it was one of the most difficult times in my life. I had no idea how to financially support my family. Without a college degree, the only job offers I was being presented with were 100 percent commission based and multi-level marketing opportunities. To say my back was up against the wall would be a huge understatement as I felt like I was, instead, pushed into the drywall and the only way to survive was to focus on my Plan "A." With my first-born son arriving in a few short months, I needed to take massive action. I was receiving unemployment, but I desperately needed a solution.

I thought at the time, when I first got into the business, that I had it figured out. I bought all the different training programs and sunk about $40,000 into that investment, so I thought I was on my way. Needless to say, I still didn't know where to start.

I don't want that to be your story. In *Find the Flipping Deals*, I want to give you access to strategies that are working right now, at the time this book was written, produced, and while it is in your hands. These are strategies that work for me and my team as well as our student investors. Do I recommend using all of these strategies? No, the way to get the most value out of this book is to choose one, two, or maybe three methods that are going to work for you. I can tell you right now; there are deals just waiting for you. You will find plenty of them using the strategies taught within this book. After years of experience, I've left no stone unturned.

I've ensured you have the full scope of tools you need so you can go out there and attain the results you desire in your business. There's a huge gap right now with individuals being able to find deals. With all the various types of training programs offered I know how it feels to not know which path to follow. I encourage you to read this book from start to finish so you can select which strategy will be the easiest for you in getting new closed transactions into your business. Don't overcomplicate what's presented in this book. If a guy like me who was voted "Least Likely to Succeed" by his high school peers can be successful in this business so can you. Right now, at the time of this writing, it is a hot, hot market. We're seeing sellers marketing their properties, and they are getting gobbled up super-fast. Investors are having a tough time finding the right types of deals to make them money.

In this book, I reveal several different strategies that you can use to find deals right now. You can get homes under contract at a great price and flip them for a nice profit (in some cases, a huge profit)! The incredible aspect of this book is that you can execute any of these strategies from literally anywhere in the entire world. You can work it 100 percent virtually if you want. The majority of what I'm going to discuss will teach you how to work from home, from your local coffee shop, while on vacation, and what I am sharing with you will apply even if you live outside of the United States.

As long as you have a strong Internet connection and a way to speak on the phone, be it through your cell or a platform like Google Voice if you live in New Zealand or Australia, for instance, you'll be ready, and able to get things rocking for yourself.

One of the brands I own is called No Flipping Excuses. The name reflects what is 100 percent true. There is literally no flipping excuse that will keep you from going out there and getting the results you want, whether that is financial freedom, spending more time with your family, buying what you want in life, or giving back. Whatever your true "why" is, you can accomplish your goals to grow your success.

Before you read further into the chapters of this book, I strongly suggest that you identify for yourself what your "why" is. You're not going to see the success you want unless you know what is driving you. Some people might strive for financial freedom. They might dream one day of going to work and telling their boss, "I quit. I'm done." They want that time and freedom that's been missing from their life.

Some people may want to know they have enough money in the bank to retire. Some people may want to have more freedom with their family, so they can take vacations, and not have to worry about a jerk of a boss saying, "You can't have those days off," and then cutting their vacation short. Nobody likes that. In my company and family, we like to give back to charity groups. When people are devastated by personal circumstances or events beyond their control, we give back to the communities and help rebuild. We let folks know they're not alone, that other folks want them to know, "We're here and we're not going anywhere." We make sure they get the help they need.

I'm going to give you not just one key but several different keys to unlock different strategies, so all you'll need to do is go through these chapters and pick out one strategy, or a handful of strategies to focus on. Once you figure it out, those will be the only strategies you need to make a massive difference in your life, and in your bank account.

I could go above and beyond and give you more proven techniques for accomplishing your end result, but I don't want to overwhelm you. Overwhelm is not something that's needed when you're learning this industry. It's a stressor, and you don't need stress in your life. So, I will give you access to all of the effective strategies we're using today in our market, so you can find the deals you want to flip. That's a significant part of this process. Once you know how to find the deals, then you just need to learn the steps to take to flip them. Use the table of contents to select what you want to learn about, and what makes that particular process work.

I'm honestly tired of seeing all the garbage out there when it comes to flipping homes. Some folks are teaching strategies that worked in the late 90s and early 2000s. It's disappointing, and that's part of the reason why I wanted to deliver completely different knowledge to you. You need to have the information that's working in the current market. Do not let this book sit on your shelf. If all you do is get past this introduction, you're setting yourself up for not seeing the results that you want and desire.

Read this book. Don't let it collect dust. Make sure you go out there and take massive action. Truly make your success happen. If you haven't read my book *Right Flipping Now*, I strongly encourage you to read it after this book. It will give you more motivation to establish your business plans and strategic moves. You will be able to lay the foundation for your own company and create a structure for yourself that lasts, not one that will collapse at the 50th floor.

I want to implore you to go out there and make your flipping plans happen. I believe everybody has the power in them to be great. You need to learn how to unleash that power and to discover your "why." Once you have your "why" it will allow you access to your full power and step into your greatness. That's your motivation. It's not me giving you a motivational speech or pep talk right before we play in the Super Bowl together. It's you, understanding what your "why" is. Once that's accomplished, you'll set yourself up to see amazing results. A lot of people never see results like the ones I'm talking about because they haven't unleashed their "why."

Thank you for getting involved with *Find the Flipping Deals*. I'm excited about the journey you're about to embark on. I've spent a lot of time and put a lot of detail into making sure you know exactly what to do with a step-by-step blueprint. That means no more guesswork for you. Instead, you can confidently execute using that blueprint every single day within your business. When you do this, you will see what will come from all your hard work.

You might have questions, right now, but be assured your questions will be answered throughout the book. If you have any questions remaining when you reach the end, I'll be more than happy to address those for you. Just send us an email, and a member of the team will promptly and cheerfully help you out. The beautiful thing about *Find the Flipping Deals* is that you're only a chapter away from closing your next deal. You're a chapter away from reaching financial freedom.

Chapter 1: The Flipping Overview

"I can accept failure, everyone fails at something. But I can't accept not trying."- Michael Jordan

Within this book, you'll find a lot of great ideas for achieving success in residential real estate. I won't cover much on commercial real estate because what I am sharing with you suits individuals wanting to work in wholesale residential properties. If you are reading this, you are likely wanting to do fix and flips, and buy properties to keep within your portfolio from a buy and hold standpoint.

The main thing that I want to discuss with you, and what you will find in later chapters, is how to find what we call "off-market" and "on-market" properties. An off-market property is a property that you can find without relying on a Multiple Listing Service (MLS) listing, LinkedIn post, YouTube notification, Facebook comment, or Craigslist ad. You will not find this property anywhere on the Internet, in a newspaper, or in an advertisement. If you can find a property using those measures, that means it is an on-market property. If the only person who knows about it is you and the individual wanting to sell their property, the owner of record, that property is considered to be off-market.

You can locate an on-market property (the opposite of an off-market property), through MLS or any other social networking platforms you can think of.

We will cover both of these types of property designations because you have an excellent opportunity right now to find off-market properties, and of course, you will need to know how to navigate on-market properties. You will have wonderful opportunities to find shadow inventory through off-market properties. But, you will also have awesome chances for instant gratification working in on-market properties because a ton of properties are still listed all over the Internet. Once you have learned as much as you can about these properties, you will see the importance in both. It will be critically important that you find one, two, or three different strategies within this book to use and that you will hone them. Make these systems your babies, and you will become a master of your craft.

I always recommend that individuals make a plan A. There is no plan B. You do not have a backup plan. You are going to make plan A work for you, and that will be the only plan that you use. People get into this business and think right away it will be just as they have seen on the webinars or infomercials on TV. They see shows like *Flip This House* and find out most of the time their experiences don't work out in the same way or equate to the same results. This is mainly because most people don't have a plan. But not you. You will be prepared because you are reading this book, and you so you will approach this endeavor in a completely different way than others who take a stab at this business. It doesn't matter if you're a novice or a veteran, what I am about to teach you will enable you to dominate in this field.

Let me reiterate; it's especially important that you focus only on your plan A. You need to keep that focus to preserve your motivation for your plan A, without the danger of plan B creeping into your mind whatsoever. Consider the story of the captain who took his crew to an island. All the ships docked at an island to go to war. But the only way to get off the island (and they didn't know this until the captain burned all the boats) was if they won so they could use their enemies' boats. There was no plan B. There was no, "Hey, if the going gets tough, we turn back. We get on the boats. We leave." So, when you go after both off-market and on-market properties, which you should do because I want you to see results as quickly as possible, determine that you will not deviate from your plan A.

Success can happen pretty quickly when you concentrate on on-market properties, and even when you deal in off-market properties. In the later chapters, you will learn the tips for finding these properties, as well as what you need to do from time-to-time to massage relationships to attract those types of deals to you. The goal is to get off-market deals under contract, so you can liquidate them as quickly as possible.

In both on and off-market properties, you will want to negotiate to the best rock bottom price available. The higher the price is discounted for you, the more that you're able to turn it for, as well as you should be able to sell it as quickly as possible, assuming that you want to go the wholesaling route. If you don't want to wholesale, you can still cut a great rehab deal or strike a worthwhile buy and hold strategy. From a wholesaling standpoint, the lower you can drive the price, the easier it will be to flip it at a discount for your end buyer.

The individuals that you will sell off-market properties to will be the individuals who have a lot of liquidity available. They can deploy acquisition capital at a moment's notice, and as long as you have the right type of deal, your property will go lightning fast. Most of the time, when you have an off-market deal or even an on-market deal that has been negotiated extremely well, and you're able to give your end buyers discounts, people will move on these properties quickly. I'm talking only 24 to 48 hours before your property is under contract, and that property is liquidated in a flash. This book is mainly designed to assist you in finding deals, which a lot of investors are having a tough time doing right now in today's market. After you digest what I am about to confide in you, any challenges in solving these problems will be overcome.

Understand, we're going to touch on what you need to know to work with cash buyers, but the main portion of this book will center around finding deals. If you need additional information to locate cash buyers, definitely check out one of our upcoming training classes at www.GetMyFlippingtraining.com. It's a free master class. You'll see how we find cash buyers who want to close on headache-free deals, without any stress. These buyers want to make your life easy, and that means *you will be* making money.

As we start diving into these chapters, make sure you pinpoint one, two, or three different strategies you can rock out to reach your complete success. Remember, there is only a plan A. There is no plan B, and there are no flipping excuses.

Chapter 2: Find the Flipping Properties

"If you're not making mistakes, then you're not doing anything. I'm positive that a doer makes mistakes." - John Wooden

Many ways exist to find deals in today's market that will yield a substantial profit, and a lot of them are just sitting there waiting for you to find them. That's why, in this chapter, we will discuss how to find great deals using the Multiple Listing Service (MLS) and why it's important that you go after pre-foreclosures, deals that are possible or potential short sales for you, and bank owned properties (REOs, probates, estate sale properties, properties that have been listed on the market for a minimum of 300 days). You'll understand why these types of deals are hidden gems, and why most people aren't going after them. Plus, I'll reveal how you can find fix and flip opportunities, better known as "handyman specials."

When I was first getting involved as a real estate investor, I debated on the best way to gain access to the MLS. I didn't want to take the path of becoming a licensed real estate agent, so I'll share with you what worked for me, the ideas I used, and the tips and tricks that you can use to gain access to the MLS.

The first step you may want to take is to become a licensed salesperson in the states where you operate. Even if it's just one state, that's fine.

Now, the reason I recommend becoming a licensed salesperson is because some of the strategies that I will explain within this chapter do require you to have access to the MLS. So, if you encounter an agent that you can't move forward with, because you don't have access to the MLS, or you are unable to meet at their office and show them the information they need to make an offer, I highly recommend you get your real estate license. Having your license will help you out dramatically, and you will unlock deals that are readily available. Your license will assist you in comping properties, and it will allow you faster access to properties.

This advice is coming from an individual who is not licensed. I see the benefits of being licensed, but I also know it's not very hard to get a license. What you have to do to obtain your license will differ from state to state, but you must complete your pre-test hours before you can take your state test. You can hold your license with a brokerage, and I would urge you to consider this option if you don't want to be a full-service real estate agent, but you want to be an investor with a license at your disposal. When you do, you will have access to the MLS. A solution to finding a brokerage is to go to a mom and pop brokerage, and just be completely upfront with them. Be transparent; you can tell them: "I'm a real estate investor, all I want to do is have access to the MLS. I will be buying and selling my properties."

If they need to take a certain commission from your deals, it will be extremely small. But in most states, all you need to do is hold your license for a year, and then you can open your own brokerage. If you are going to be the only person in business, then the brokerage would reside solely with you. If you do make this decision, be aware that you will need an additional disclosure on the majority of your agreements. Make sure you talk to an attorney who can advise you on what you need to include in your agreements.

You can also become an assistant to a licensed salesperson within the state, or states, where you operate. This will allow you access to the MLS, and to comp properties, and it will also permit you to make offers on properties. The only thing it won't allow you to do is look at properties because you won't be an actual salesperson; you won't have what's called a century key card. You can't just head over and look at properties because you need to be a licensed salesperson to do that. Typically, this access will run you anywhere between $300 to $500 for the year, so it is a smart business expense you can write off, and it's a phenomenal investment for the year.

You just have to find the right type of real estate agent who is willing to allow this type of relationship, and there has to be a mutual benefit for them to work with you. When you approach them, I would let the agent know whenever you come across deals that you might do a fix and flip, or you might find a deal to wholesale. If you're working a rehabber, make sure that you at least give that rehabber your agent's information, so they can potentially list the property. The more business you bring to them, the longer the relationship will flourish. When that happens, your business will continue to grow.

The next thing that I would recommend is to work with your agent in person. They can perform the searches discussed in this chapter. You might go their office, meet them at a coffee shop, or they could come to your home office or your office suite. The strategies applicable to this chapter, and that I recommend you implement can be used when you are sitting right next to your agent, allowing you to elaborate to them exactly what you want to be done.

The only thing I would not recommend doing, especially if you're working with an agent who gives you access to their MLS, is using their login credentials. They can get in trouble, especially with the MLS security system monitoring who's logging into their account from anywhere in the world. That information can be gathered quickly. So be careful. Don't get your agent into trouble; they are a really great resource to have, and the business relationship could quickly thrive if you and your agent do things the right way.

The recommendation here is not to grab their login credentials and enter the site yourself. If you don't plan on getting your license and you would prefer to be an assistant to a salesperson or to work with an agent, you don't want the agent to get in trouble by abusing their credentials.

Within this chapter, we are going to examine some very particular deals. When it comes to finding deals on the MLS, we want to search for active deals. You'll see, once you have logged in to the MLS, specific listings called AcT; that stands for active properties. You will also note a listing type of ACT, which uses a capital C. When you see this, it means the property's active, but the seller is openly accepting counters, and they're also openly accepting backup offers. This means there is an opportunity for you to make a backup offer. However, you will often find this is a waste of time.

Go after active properties without the contingency of your offer being a backup. Depending on your area, you may want to pursue single-family residences, as compared to both single-family and condominiums. I mention this because when you are on the MLS, you will see the two categories are lumped into one search criteria. So, be clear and check off if you want to find only single-family residences, which is my recommendation. Again, I'm in a totally different market. It's true, I also invest in other markets, and I do know that some markets are piping hot when it comes to condominiums. It's important to know your market. You need to know what is selling. Knowing what will help your properties quickly and easily will be the difference maker and you'll see bigger profit checks at the closing table.

Select the areas you want to invest in. For example, on most multiple listing services you will see a section that will ask you for the areas you want to target. I typically go after the top five areas where the most cash transactions have been completed, and where I see the most potential. I like to look at those areas because, usually, if I find a property within that area that I can negotiate at a rock-bottom price, it will probably be flipped quickly, due to how hot the area is.

A great indication of how in-demand a market is will result after you do your due diligence to determine what properties are selling, how they're selling and the number of days they sit on the market on average. When you analyze areas in this way, you will get a strong indicator of whether you want to deal there. Identify your top five, and you will find plenty of eligible properties to work with.

When you are doing these searches for active properties, you need to gauge where most of the transactions are happening, in relation to the price range. Look at it from a listing standpoint and go after certain price ranges. If you notice a lot of the transactions are $300,000 or less, those are your prime properties. If you're not seeing a lot of activity at $300,000 or above, it probably wouldn't make sense to consider those types of properties, unless you can negotiate them at a deep, deep discount.

One of the key takeaways I want you to have is that you can find different types of properties. To get started I recommend looking under the disclosures section of the MLS platform; this will allow you to search what kind of properties you've pinpointed. Let's say you want to go after distressed properties, aka properties that have been served what's called a "lis pendens," or a notice of default. This means the owner of record has gone four months delinquent, or more, on their particular subject property, which warrants the property to be in what's called a "pre-foreclosure stage." If you want to find these types of properties, look for what's called "short sale possible," or a "pre-foreclosure," under the disclosures section on the MLS.

The cool advantage of short sales is you can find properties that have already been approved by the bank. In what's called the "Agent to Agent Remarks Section," you could read notes from the actual listing agent. For example, I'm reviewing a listing right now that says, "Bank approved short sale, approval will be obtained within 48 to 72 business hours." The listing goes on to provide the information for the real estate agent. It states: "Offers must include proof of funds, and/or preapproval letter." If you need to obtain a proof of funds letter, you can get it at besttransactionfunding.com. They know exactly what you will need and will give you a specific proof of funds letter, so you can move forward with your transaction.

The MLS gives you a great opportunity to find already-approved short sales, so you can see what the number is and if you will be even close to the offer you want to put in. On properties that don't have approvals already, it's an open game. You can put in whatever offer you want; just make sure it's not a completely low-ball offer because most of the time those offers will not be accepted. By the time you find out your offer was rejected, it's more than likely that another offer will have come in, and that one will get accepted. So, make sure you're coming in at your maximum allowable offer, anywhere between 65 to 80 percent of the after-repair value. Those numbers obviously depend on your market.

You can also transact estate sale properties. Estate sale properties have proven to be lucrative vehicles for investors going after executors managing the estate of a person who has recently passed away. In most cases, executors want to liquidate their property as quickly as possible. Meaning, most of the time when you see estate sale properties pop up on the MLS, you know it will prove to be a sound opportunity for you to help solve a problem for the executor and the heirs of the estate. Sometimes, an estate is managed by an attorney, in partnership with the real estate agent. When you find that type of arrangement, it could be a valuable opportunity to come in and negotiate a rock bottom price on the estate.

In some instances, you can also negotiate for the entire estate, which can include furniture inside the house, any collectibles, and even cars. Because it can include more than just the property, I always write into my purchase and sales agreements that the estate is to be included. When you do this, you simply need to specify what items you would like to have remain in the subject property. Many estate properties can be approved quickly, as most have already gone through the process of probate court—which can be a lengthy process if you begin negotiations right at the beginning, or if the executor is waiting for certain documentation to be approved by the judge–for instance.

Bank owned, and foreclosed properties are properties the bank has already sent to auction. The bank has bought back the properties, and the previous owners have already received notice of default, their lis pendens. This property has gone through the whole judicial or non-judicial process for that particular sate, and now the bank owns the property. The properties that are listed right now on the MLS are properties that the banks want to liquidate at normally a substantial discount. I just did an MLS search in the five areas where I want to buy, and it returned 108 matches. That's amazing because it means that's 108 opportunities I could make offers on.

Will that be the routine result for every market across the country? Probably not. That's a middle of the range for particular areas where my team and I want to invest. Indianapolis, one of the areas where we do invest, isn't the largest of metropolitan cities, so what returned, I know is a relatively normal number. But again, your results will vary depending on where in the country you are searching.

Now, let's discuss the meaning of "days on the market." When you start your searches, you will read that some properties have been on the MLS for a very long time. Most of the time, this means that investors don't want to do enough due diligence to get these properties under contract. They might submit offers and hope they get approved, but they won't many times because the person making the offer didn't take the time to talk to the real estate agent about the property. They were rejected because they didn't find out the needs of the owner of record on the subject property.

This situation can be avoided if you just find out some simple information. Once you have dug into the property a bit, then if it makes sense, you can submit an offer. I always encourage individuals to look at the subject property, to put forth that you really do want the property. When you take this extra step, it gives great feedback to the owner and instills in them the confidence that you have a high interest in their home. Maybe the numbers will be a little bit off, but at least, when you visit the home in-person, the owner knows that you're serious, as compared to submitting an offer sight unseen and hoping that it gets approved.

If you are interested in finding properties that have been on the market for a long time, you might see what's called a "C" in front of the "D" in "Days on Market." This means there's been some sort of change between when the property was listed and the current date you are looking at the property on the market. The property could have been listed for $200,000, but then maybe six months went by, and the owner of record told the agent, "I think we need to do a price decrease and lower it to $190,000." The listing will still reflect the six months, but it (somewhat) restarts at the new list price, at zero days. You can review this at a glance, but when agents click into the details of the property, they will see it's been listed for the six months. They will also see the difference in price, and the CDOM (cumulative days on market) on the particular property.

These properties are a sweet find! If you want to find the days on the market in a property search you will need to–or have a real estate agent–add an extra section on the MLS called DOM, as most real estate agents do not have access to this function with their pre-configured software through the MLS. It means you are given access to a brand-new section to search for properties specifically being listed on the market for an extended period of time. All MLS sites vary from each other, but all will also run almost in the same website format as most of the MLS platforms that are operating today.

No matter the MLS system you use, you'll find the search engines and listings are pretty much the same across the board. If you want to find a special fixer-up property, you won't be able to see it easily. That information won't be readily available, but you can usually find it toward the bottom of the main MLS page. That specification is called "Disclosure Other." Select "Fixer Upper," and properties that may need new roofs, electricity, plumbing or carpets will be returned. You won't know what the property requires until you dive in and read the "Agent to Agent Remarks" section, which denotes the repairs that specific property needs.

You will also be able to find probate properties within the Disclosure section on the main MLS page. You won't find a whole lot of them, because most of the time when probates are listed, it's as a last resort for the executor to try and liquidate the estate. We will cover probates in a later chapter, and I will share with you how to find probates before they hit the actual MLS.

Top tips for closing deals: 1) Make sure you contact the listing agent. Have a conversation with them about the property. Discuss the property, especially if it's been listed for a long period of time, or if it's a short sale. Find out as many details as possible, like if any offers were recently submitted, and what happened with them. Sometimes you'll discover that an offer was accepted, but the individual who wrote the offer couldn't get their financing. So, the offer fell through and now it's back on the market, readily available. When that happens, a listing will usually go to active C, which means it's a contingency with a backup offer. Because there are all kinds of different transactional situations, it's always a wise idea to find out what's going on with the property, and how you can be a problem solver.

That leads me to tip number 2) Find out the motivation for why the sellers are selling. You could find that information from the real estate agent; they're not doing anything to violate their fiduciary responsibility by disclosing why the property is on the market. They can't obviously disclose price, or the lowest the sellers would be able to accept—that would be a big violation—but it is always pertinent to try and find out the motivation behind why the property has been listed.

Tip number 3) Look at the property. If you can't make it out to the location, you can have a team member go on your behalf and give the listing agent feedback. As discussed, when you take this step, you will really emphasize that you do have interest in the property. You may have to go out to the property two or three times to get comfortable with your price and have it approved by the owners of record. As is the case with any property, you never really know what you are getting into until you physically view the property and start finding out the whys.

Tip 4) Find out from the listing agent if the sellers are willing to come off the current listing price. Again, we don't want them to violate their fiduciary responsibility, which more than likely they won't, but it is vital to find out, if a property is listed for $190,000, for instance, if the sellers are willing to accept any number other than the listing price. Set realistic expectations with the agent. You will either hear a yes or no; they agent won't say, "Yes, they'll come down $10,000, $15,000, $20,000." But you can say, "I want to put an offer in, but I'm not sure if it's going to meet what you guys are asking for, so before I do that and potentially waste anybody's time, is there any way you could tell me if the list price is firm, or are they flexible?" This has been the best way I have found to handle such situations.

Finally, tip 5) Make sure you explain to the listing agent why you want to buy the property and then have the listing agent explain your reasoning to the sellers. The more they know, the better. If they hear, "This individual is going to come buy the property. They're part of an investment group. They want to fix up the property and turn it into a great family home, then market it to sell it, not rent it, to an actual family," that information goes a long way. I would encourage you to share your intention with the agent.

Before we close this chapter, and as a bonus for you, because I really want to make sure you have your bases covered to find the right types of deals, let's dissect what makes a sweet spot a sweet spot for investor buyers. You want to find areas where you can see lots of properties closing with either cash investors or financed buyers. The shorter the properties were listed on the market, the more ideal. I personally like to see properties within 30 days or less. You'll be able to see a solid mixture of cash transactions within the areas you're buying in, so you will see properties that have had financing associated with them. You could also see what's called 1031 exchanges—which we won't get into in this book, but if you are curious, you can find out everything you need to know about 1031 exchanges by simply doing a Google search.

When you weigh the benefits and drawbacks of your properties, don't forget to factor in the days on market. That number should be low, because if properties are moving fast that's a big key indication that you can get those properties sold rapidly. When I conduct my searches, I want to see properties that are selling for a decent amount. If I go into the MLS right now and explore my top five areas, I will see anywhere between 90 to 320 recently-sold cash transactions within the last three to four months. Anything below that number is not a good indicator for you for that market. Note that you will see a mixture of both financed and cash transactions, and from those, you will want to find your target sweet spot, with prices that most individuals are buying at.

In certain areas of Indianapolis, our sweet spots are $150,000 and below. Some areas are going to be $300,000 or below. As we've talked about, it just all depends on the area; that's why it's important to do your due diligence. When you are assessing properties, go no further back than three to four months at the absolute max, unless you're in a rural area, then I would go as far as two years back. This will allow you to find the supporting data you need to know where to price your properties. This information will help you out exponentially when it comes to getting your properties sold. The more data you gather, the shorter period of time you will have to hold onto your properties, the fewer times you will spend wondering if you'll be able to get the properties you have under contract liquidated.

The last thing you want to do is not close on multiple properties. That means egg on your face, and it doesn't turn out to be a great day for you. The goal is to put your properties under contract and get them sold within 24 to 48 hours; that's the ideal way to sell properties.

As you continue, keep it fresh in your mind that you will need to find your one to three strategies within this book. When you select your strategies, don't be afraid to really go gung-ho with them. You're going to find great deals on the MLS; most investors want to feel instant gratification when a deal is accepted under contract, and you'll have the tools to liquidate it. One of the best ways to do that is through your access to the MLS.

Chapter 3: Flipping HUDs

"It always seems impossible until it's done." - Nelson Mandela

In this chapter, I'm going to discuss how to flip several HUD properties per month virtually from any market. You'll learn the full details of the listing periods, the language you need to know, why HUD homes are such a great opportunity for purchasing properties at great discounts, and how to properly bid on HUD homes, a bidding process you need to become quite familiar with. I'll go over examples of HUD deals and discuss performing due diligence. I'm also giving you a transactional funder to fund your HUD deals for you.

Let's discuss the listing periods first. On the HUD Home Store website, there are several types of listings periods. The lottery period runs seven days and applies to both insured and uninsured HUD listed properties. The lottery period has a program called the "Good Neighbor Next Program" only for insured HUD homes which allows law enforcement, pre-K through 12th-grade teachers, firefighters, and EMTs to purchase HUD properties at half off the list price. The lottery period for listed uninsured HUD properties allows non-profits, government entities, and "Good Neighbor Next

Program" buyers to place bids to purchase during the seven-day period. Exclusive properties allow for absolutely no investor bidding. Insured properties will be exclusive for a period of 15 days. Once the lottery period has concluded the exclusive period begins. This period allows owner-occupant buyers to place bids. This is for people that plan on living in the property for a minimum of one-year before they can sell the home.

The next listing period is the extended period, which we'll discuss momentarily. Uninsured exclusive properties are only listed for five days. What this means is that all uninsured properties enter a five-day exclusive period after the lottery period. The next listing period is the extended period. This is the period a property enters after the lottery and exclusive periods have passed.

During this period, you are allowed to start making bids at any point in time and investors will come in and start bidding as well. The difference between this period and the exclusive is that you can still bid on exclusive for HUD homes if you're planning on owning the property, which means you will become an owner-occupant. You have to live in the property and make it your primary residence. If you bid on extended properties, you are doing so as an investor, meaning, you are not planning on making this home your primary residence.

Another listing applies to owners of non-profits. You will have a certain period of time to act, called the dollar listings. This criterion is used for government purchases only. This listing period is 10 days and is relevant to homes that have an as-is appraisal value of $1 to $25. After the dollar listing period, the home enters an extended listing period that has no ending date, except when the home has been purchased or reanalyzed. Government agencies can still purchase the home for $1 after the homes leave the dollar listing period and enter the extended listing period. If you have a non-profit, you are eligible to bid on the dollar homes. All you need to do is enter your non-profit's information.

Let's talk about the language that you need to know. IE stands for "insurable with repair escrow." Simplified, the property requires repairs estimated to cost no more than $5,000. It is eligible for a FHA-insured loan, provided the purchaser's lending sets up a repair escrow at closing. IN on the HUD Home Store site stands for "insurable," meaning the property is eligible for an FHA-insured loan in its current condition. UI stands for "uninsured." By definition, the property requires an estimated cost of more than $5,000 in repairs. It is not eligible for an FHA insured loan unless a section 203k loan can be arranged.

Let's discuss why HUD homes are a viable option, although many realtors don't like selling them because they either don't understand the process, they aren't motivated by the limited commissions, or they don't like filling out the paperwork. A lot of times they don't have the buyers. This really boils down to having buyers that can't get approved if the repairs are needed. You will want to make sure you have investors at your disposal, because investors can buy these properties without inspection. They're not getting appraisals or financing. They can just come in and purchase the home, and many real estate agents don't have investors within their network.

HUD homes give you instant equity. If you bid on them right, you could actually make a lot of equity. We'll go over the specific strategy you can use for the bidding process shortly. HUD homes also have no deed restrictions. Unlike short sales that, in most cases, do require deed restrictions,

HUD differs. Some states have very limited competition. This is mainly due to not understanding the HUD process.

Before you start bidding, be prepared to encounter listing and value errors. Often, agents and/or the asset managers associated with the subject property will input listings with errors. They might get the square footage, bedrooms, bathrooms, or the lot size wrong. We'll discuss later in this chapter how these typos can equal a discount in your favor.

Let's cover how to properly bid on HUD homes. For the purposes of illustration, we'll use sample figures for our initial starting point. You will likely not enter in information and win the bid right off the bat. You will first simply want to get the process started, so you can establish a starting point to set the algorithm on the HUD Home Store's website.

For a two-bedroom property, you're going to use a 37 percent net to HUD. For example, if the home is listed at $100,000, in order for it to close in this particular example, HUD would need to net $37,000. A three-bedroom property would be 47 percent net to HUD. A four-bedroom and beyond will be at 57 percent net to HUD. Once you figure that starting point, then you can solve where HUD will come in. As we progress within this chapter, you'll know what to do with your counter-offers as well.

On hudhomestore.com enter the state you want to purchase in and make sure under buyer type that you enter "investor." Doing so will show you all the properties currently available in the areas you've selected.

Once listings appear within your specified areas, click on them to read the information about the properties. You'll receive the subject address, bedroom and bath count, total rooms, square feet and the year the property was built. You will see whether it's a single family with an attached or detached garage. The list price will be visible, and you can also see if it's eligible for a 203k loan.

There's a special tab on the specific listing called agent info that lists the asset manager and the listing broker. This information is important because, if you're not a real estate agent yourself, you will need to have your real estate agent enter the bids. If any communication needs to happen between either the asset manager or the listing broker of the subject property, that information will be readily available on all listings on HUD Home Store. You can see where all the properties are, and if you want to check out the homes on Trulia or Zillow, the properties will be listed there also.

If your agent's bidding for you, it will automatically calculate what the listing broker will receive for commission. This amount will typically be the same commission amount no matter what agent you use, but I highly encourage you to use your own agent and not the listing broker.

In section 5, when you're filling out your HUD bidding information, you will need to insert an actual number, and here, you will enter a zero. You'll read: "The seller will pay reasonable and customary costs but not more than actual cost, nor more than paid by a typical seller in the area of obtaining financing and/or closing in any amount not to exceed." If you're not familiar with exactly what that is, it's basically seller concession. We're not asking for any type of seller concession or consideration, so that is why you would type in the zero.

As you scroll down the specific page, record that you are buying the property as an investor. I always have our offers held as a backup just in case they are not accepted immediately. The reason why is because the owner may come back to you at a later point in time, so you want to prepare for that possibility. It's usually a positive sign.

I never buy properties in my company name because if I buy it in my regular name using my Social Security number, we get a better deal. The owner sees an individual buying the property versus a business entity, and that is usually preferable. You may want to speak to an attorney for the best way to handle your purchase, but we use this tactic frequently and it serves us well.

Once you purchase the property, if your end game is to sell it immediately and execute what's called an A to B, B to C, transaction, your first transaction can be completed under your individual sole proprietor name. Then you could quit claim it as soon as you buy it and put it into a business entity and sell it to your end buyer.

When a property is accepted by HUD, you have two business days to get the paperwork to the listing broker. They'll verify everything and then, if everything is in order, your offer will be accepted. You can then execute and purchase the property. Since we have a pretty decent wholesaling operation, we wholesale a lot of our HUD properties. Timing has a lot to do with the success of the deal.

For instance, if you win a bid on a Friday, that means you'll have all day Friday, Saturday, Sunday, and until the end of the business day Monday, to come up with your earnest money deposit. Your real estate agent will also have that same block of time to confirm certain HUD documents are signed. The documents are to be signed and delivered before the specified deadline in your particular area.

Several different types of bid statuses exist: the sealed bid, pending review, under review, accepted, other bid selected, other bid under contract, canceled, and withdrawn. Once you make your bids, you will be able to see your status. Most of the time as soon as you click submit, the property will be updated to read "SB," which stands for sealed bid. You'll receive a response within about 24 hours usually. Once you note "sealed bid," you want to keep a watch on the property because a new label might populate called "OBS," referring to "other bid selected, or canceled."

Review your bids daily because HUD will respond. If you have a counter, then you want to either accept or counter back. Once you have received a response from HUD, the status will be updated to canceled. If you check your canceled bids you will see a counteroffer bid button. These changing statuses are why you want to check in on your bids often. As the status changes, you will have the information you need so you can move your deal forward.

Next, take a look at the list price and compare that to your bid amount. Then review what HUD is specifically asking for. You will receive responses from HUD quite a bit and it's a lot of back and forth because you're dealing with an algorithm. This is why you want to deal with these transactions in the proper manner. We'll discuss how to handle your counteroffers in a later section of this chapter.

Before we get into the nuts and bolts of comprehending the counteroffer, let's assume we have a case where we do receive a counter, and it's way off from where we need to be for our property. We always round up our bid to the nearest $50. We do that because we might trigger the HUD Home Store's algorithm they use for accepting, canceling, or countering offers. If we use the $50 rule of thumb a few times, we might get our offer accepted.

Now HUD may elect to accept, cancel, or counter your offers. If HUD is close to 70 percent net, then we'll increase our bid by $50 to $100. Remember, it's important to select numbers that will make you money. You obviously don't want to keep bidding just to get a bid accepted, because if it doesn't make sense to you, it's not going to make sense. It's best not to waste people's time.

Here's a key bonus. After a property has been listed for longer than a 90-day period, we will bid every single day, usually increasing our offer by $50 increments depending on how badly we want the property. We've seen substantial discounts on properties that have been on HUD Home Store for longer than 90 days.

You should have a clear expectation of what you need to do for your due diligence. You can refer to what's called the "property condition report" (PCR). I'll talk about where you can find this data as well as another report—the repair escrow document—on the HUD Home Store as we get further into the process.

Your next step is to perform a county search on the property. Double check Google for the county information and to locate the assessor's office to find out specific details on the property. You can also determine another opinion of value, through the use of MLS comps, RealQuest, Eppraisal, Zillow, realtor.com, and Trulia. Double check the property descriptions closely because you will discover there are always errors in HUD listings. Tax assessor information is invaluable for determining discrepancies.

Make sure you compare the property condition report as well. Pay close attention to items like the roof, foundation, furnace, HVAC unit, electrical panel, plumbing and if there is any visible mold. Issues in these areas could drastically change the way you bid.

Observe the neighborhood closely. Drive through it to find out if there are any nearby schools, parks, and hospitals. The presence of these entities may increase the value and entice future buyers or tenants for the property.

You can also ask neighbors about the house. Neighbors are always more than happy to share details on the property, which could expose a lot, any major concerns, foundation issues, or any environmental problems. HUD may not know the true state of the property, but you definitely need to. If

HUD doesn't know the scoop, then they might not be able to properly disclose it.

A home inspection is always recommended with your HUD properties. Even though you're buying the property in as-is condition, it's still a smart move. If you're wholesaling the property, then the inspection is up to your buyer because the buyer is purchasing in an as-is condition. A home inspection will protect you and your future buyer from major money repairs, so don't close unless your inspection is actually complaint. If you are purchasing, wholesaling and selling in as-is condition, it is fine to proceed forward without an inspection, but if you're buying the property as a rehab, I would not move forward unless a home inspection has been performed.

To find all the information you need for your property, go back onto the HUD Home Store under the specific subject property listings. Find a tab called addendums, which will contain everything you want to know about the property, such as bidding and escrow information, earnest money guidelines, and the property conditions report. I highly advise you to get your PCR, as it is a key element to your HUD deal.

If you are looking for a company to help fund your deals, I recommend besttransactionfunding.com for all your transactions. These individuals are especially effective to work with if you're looking to do an A to B, B to C, transaction. Simply go to their website and fill out their intake form. In about three business days they will have your deal funded and you can anticipate receiving your cut at closing. Using this company gives you a superior strategy because they don't require the use of your own credit or cash. The individuals are phenomenal to work with. We use them all the time, and a lot of our student investors use them as well. I highly encourage you to do the same.

This is a really great strategy to use for finding and purchasing your HUD homes. Because HUD does release properties on a daily basis, implementing this funding recommendation simply makes sense and will give you a definite advantage. If you're not the real estate agent keeping an eye out for counteroffers, make sure you have a really solid relationship with your real estate agent. Let them know they're going to need to keep watching for changes, especially counters, to your property every day. You do not want to miss out on an opportunity. If you receive a counteroffer from HUD, you need to act quickly. As I mentioned, they typically will respond within 24 hours, not including Saturday or Sunday. If you bid on a Monday, for example, you will probably receive an answer either before the end of the business day (depending on when you made the bid), or first thing the following day.

For people who want to go all-in, I encourage you to explore this route. You work HUD deals in addition to maybe one or two other strategies because doing so will allow you to close one to two deals a month, depending on your market. Once you are comfortable with that arrangement, you can implement one more strategy, so you will be able to close between four to six deals every single month.

Chapter 4: What the Flip is Zillow?

"Our greatest weakness lies in giving up. The most certain way to succeed is always to try just one more time." -
Thomas A. Edison

You may have heard of Zillow. It's a website that gives you a lot of ways to find properties, real estate agents and people in the mortgage business. When you use Zillow, the main thing you will want to do is find properties at a discount. If your main strategy for purchasing is finding properties at a great rate, you can use Zillow. You can purchase these properties at a good price, with potentially no rehab, and a nice cash flow when you have the right type of tenant.

Zillow allows you to find properties at discounts, lease-options, short sales and even income-producing properties. You can spin Zillow to your advantage in a lot of cool ways.

On Zillow's home page, enter the area where you want to invest. In my case, I would type in "Indianapolis, Indiana" and see what populates. I can see, when I do that, there are 3,476 homes for sale. Now, we don't want to go after all of those homes. That's far too many, and a lot of these homes will be listed for retail by real estate agents. There is probably not a lot of wiggle room unless you want to purchase those properties for a unique reason such as to turn them into income-producing properties.

One of the features that I love about Zillow is that we can circle and hover over "listing type." When we click on "listing type," a dropdown box will appear giving us several options. Check out "for sale" and the various arrangements: "by agents," "by owner," "new construction," "foreclosures" and "coming soon." Uncheck "by agents," "new construction," "foreclosures" and "coming soon."

The second category on the dropdown is "potential listings." We don't want any of these, so we can uncheck that box. Now, my search has been narrowed to pull up homes I want to look at and that leaves me with 153 homes out of the 3,000 plus that originally appeared. These are completely at my disposal. Let's start finding exactly the kind of properties we want by going over to the next box where it says, "any price." Typically for Indianapolis, we see a max price of $250,000, so I'm going to enter that in, and then click "enter." I see 125 homes and I don't think that's much of a difference, which tells me I have a pretty accurate return. I know these are most of the homes in Indianapolis, and they will be the properties we are most interested in.

Now, we do likely want a particular number of bedrooms, so you can also clarify that detail. In this particular instance, I'm going to look at two-plus bedroom homes and the home type. I'll type in the home type, of "houses," and Zillow gives us the configuration to select "houses," "apartments," "condominiums," "townhomes" and "manufactured homes." You can also look for lots and land. I'm going to uncheck "apartments," "condominiums," "townhomes," "manufactured homes" and "lots" and "land," because I'm only looking for residential properties for this particular search.

But you can use completely different filters for your search and seek properties anywhere in the entire world. Next, we'll consider bathrooms. We want most of our properties to have at least one bath. So, let's indicate that. You don't need to do anything else in the "more" section unless you have specific cash buyers or investors looking for a minimum square footage or properties built within a certain year. If your cash buyers have specified they only want to look at properties built 1992 or newer, or 1,000 square feet or newer construction; this is a great way for you to narrow down your search.

Whatever you plug into Zillow really depends on what you're looking to do. I'm reviewing 95 homes that have popped up. I've taken the results from 135 to 95 homes that fit our needs. And I want to look at the cheapest homes. So, I can address the section on Zillow, right under where it says "Indianapolis, Indiana, for sale by owner" and click on "cheapest properties," to ensure I will see all the properties that are extremely cheap.

The first one here is listed for $7,500 and it's for sale by owner. There is no picture of the home; I can only see the address and an overview of the most pertinent points of the property. If I click on the property, then I will see a new page that will contain the actual property profile. The list price is $7,500, but the Zestimate says $34,017. But I want to ask myself before I go any further, *how much do I believe the property is worth $34,000?* From what we can tell as real estate investors, and what I know from coaching thousands of students over the years, and compiled information, the Zestimate is not accurate. It's very inaccurate, in fact. You will want to determine the Zestimates on your own properties and because I know sometimes the numbers don't add up, I would not rely on that amount 100 percent.

If you want to get a general gauge for what properties are close to in price, that's fine. I would say in terms of the property we're discussing, the $34,000 Zestimate is not a good figure. I would venture for $7,500 since it's more than likely going to be about 80 percent of that price, which is about $27,000. We're roughly a few thousand dollars off. Once the Zestimate question has been satisfied, I will move over to the property descriptions. This gives me everything I need to know. Our particular property is at 737 West 32nd Street; it's a two bedroom one-bath home; the square footage is 1,020, and we can read a description of the property stating:

"This two bed, one-bath home has a lot of potential. Half the home is gutted; the house has a new 200-amp electric panel and service entry cable installed in fall of 2016. There is also a bonus one-bedroom, one-bath with living room and kitchen apartment at the back of the property separate from the house to give rental income to the property. It's an amazing property for the price, listed at only $16,737."

It appears the price has been decreased, because you'll remember the original price of $7,500. The year built is 1920, so it's an older home. As we scroll down, we can find out even more information like the price and task history. We can also read they've been trying to sell the property for a long time.

This leads us to the next stage of the process and one you don't want to skip. I recommend you find out motivation for the sale before you call the individual listed. This is always a smart chore. As I dig deeper, I see the tax assessment for this property is at $13,500, but because I know the area, and that they slash the assessment value in half in Marion County, Indiana, I can figure this property is pretty close to my original assessment of $27,000. Put it another way: $13,500 x 2 gives me that value even before I read the property description that stated it was practically gutted.

All factors considered, we might be able to get this property at a pretty good deal. And an awesome function of Zillow, when you're looking at the tax history, is that it has a tab that permits you to find tax assessment information on the county website. From there you can find out the current owner of record, and this helps when you make your phone call to the seller. If you are scanning the "for sale by owner" listings on Zillow, when you go to the right-hand side, you will have access to view a section that reads "get more information." Simply fill out your name, phone number and email, and then you can click the blue button that says "contact." This is a point of entry to find the actual seller information.

As you scroll down, you'll notice realtor information. On the listing we're learning about, there are three realtors evident, but move further down the page and "property owner" comes into view. The property owner section will have the phone number listed for this individual who is the owner of record. All you need to do is give them a call to learn if they are looking to sell the property quickly. If they are open to your time frame and conditions, you could potentially get the property at a much larger discount than its current listed price on Zillow.

You can instantly locate properties owned by individuals who want to quickly liquidate their properties. These listings will tell you everything you need to know to make a sensible decision. Once you start using Zillow frequently, you'll be pleased with how fast you can put in a phone call to the owners.

Before you call, double check the individual is not on a do not call list. A safer way to proceed than calling directly, especially since they have given their information out, is to automate the calling process. Because there are 95 listings for our particular search example, it makes more sense and saves more time to hire a virtual assistant. You can find a virtual assistant (VA) on upwork.com; they can gather the data from the properties you're interested in once a week and input it.

I set up a Google Sheet for properties and the owners of record that is updated once a week. Properties are advertised in groups and they are consistently loaded up on Zillow daily, weekly and monthly. Make sure your VA allows the Google Sheet to be shared between the two of you, and they can also be tasked with inputting all the property information, such as the street number, street name, city, state, zip code, how many bedrooms, how many baths, the square footage, current asking price, the Zestimate and year built of the property as well as other details you desire to help you negotiate.

It would be good to know that half the home has been gutted, as we've been talking about. I definitely would not want to leave that critical detail out. My VA can put that property status in the notes section on my spreadsheet.

Once we've recorded the property information and owner contact details on the Google Sheet, we can take all the phone numbers and enter them onto another sheet, via copy and paste. I like to enter that data into Slybroadcast and then schedule a message to go out to the property contacts.

The message could be quite simple and sound like this: "Hey, my name's Jason Lucchesi, I saw that you had a property listed on Zillow and I wanted to give you call because I'm very interested in it. I'm a real estate investor and we have cash ready to close on properties. So, please give me a call back at 123-456-789." That's it, all you need to do to leave a message through Slybroadcast. This is very efficient because people include their contact information on Zillow, and that message can go out to each of them. Recording the message and sending it out takes one minute to do. Once you send it out, people start calling you.

If the property is still available, people are going to call you and want to talk with you about their property. After you gather important facts about the home, you can decide if you are still intrigued enough to put in an offer. It's useful to have your Google Sheet in front of you because you will have many properties to keep track of and you want to impress upon people that you know what you're talking about. Without the sheet, you might wind up sounding like: "Oh yeah, I called quite a few people. Can you tell me which property you're at and the property that you're selling please?" When you're informed you let people know you definitely want to know the property and you want as much information on it as possible, so you can make a good offer.

We've covered what's called the "One Call Close" on our *No Flipping Excuses* podcast show. You can learn how to conduct yourself on that call absolutely for free on iTunes. Just search "No Flipping Excuses," under podcasts, and our show will pull up for you. That episode, titled "The One Call Close," is one of the more popular ones we've aired to-date. I strongly advise you to listen to it, especially if you're looking for advice and information on the best practices of what to say when doing these types of calls.

When you get the "One Call Close" down to a science it can nab you an extra one, two, or three-plus deals monthly with the potential to make you from $5,000, $10,000 or $15,000 because Zillow is one of the largest search engines for real estate and constantly lists properties for you to work. If you need a real estate agent, you can also find good ones on Zillow. All you need to do when you're looking for an agent is go to "agent finder," and when you do that, it will populate everything. Specifically, if I were already searching in Indianapolis, Indiana, it would pull up "Indianapolis, Indiana real estate agents," and I could research the agents to decide if I want to work with them.

You can also find home improvement individuals, property managers, builders, inspectors, photographers, and other tradespeople. So, if you're trying to build out your team, which if you've read my book *Right Flipping Now*, you know I advise as a tactic and a huge component of your success. Building out your team means you can eliminate yourself from doing every job in the business; you can even remove yourself from the manual dealings and have your team execute while you assume a CEO role. As a CEO, you should be focusing on building the business rather than being *in* the business stuck on the first floor.

Zillow provides a huge opportunity to find a lot of the right people you need for your real estate investing business. The database is simple and straightforward, giving you easy access to owners of record so you can start making phone calls and offers. Remember, I highly encourage you to make 15 offers each and every week. That equates to 60 offers every month. Make sure those offers are quality. When you commit to following through on that level of volume it will only help you to close more deals.

Sixty offers presented, equals two to three, possibly even four deals closed every single month. That's the goal you want to reach, and the exciting fact is that the results you desire are right around the corner. Whenever you are ready, you can start calling folks on Zillow and begin closing lucrative properties.

Chapter 5: Build Your Flipping Team

"Never give up, for that is just the place and time that the tide will turn." - Harriet Beecher Stowe

One of the most important relationships you can have is with individuals that not only can help you with your business but who you could also help in their business. This chapter will cover the keys you can use in certain relationships that are going to help you secure the deals you need. Now, if you've read my previous book, I've talked about the importance of having an investor-friendly attorney, using an investor-friendly title company to close your transactions, as well as working with investor-friendly real estate agents, contractors and bird dogs.

You need quite a few people to help you structure your business, so it will revolve around enabling you to work in the business constantly. These people can also become key players on your team and can create constant deals in your pipeline. One key relationship we're going to discuss in this chapter that a lot of investors overlook is an insurance agent. Think about it. If something happens to a home, who will be the first to receive notification of anything wrong with the property?

When I'm talking to an insurance agent, I like to confirm they are going to be the first to get a notification if somebody wants to sell. The main reason this happens is because of their policy. If I am a homeowner and I want to sell my property, I'll let my insurance agent know, "We're going to be putting the house on the market. We're probably not going to be on the policy that much longer." The seller will also want to know from the insurance agent, since they paid for a year in advance, if they will get a portion of that payment back.

You want about 3-5 insurance agents on your team. Depending on where you live, some areas might have more prevalent hail damage than others, for example. But a lot of the times, if people are in an area where hail damage is very prevalent, and they receive a lot of damage to their property, it may be worth their time to move instead of repairing the property.

If there's a lot of damage to the side of the house, or to the roof, they may want to leave. We've seen this happen a few times where damage was sustained, and the homeowners received a check to do the repairs, but they decided to move instead. If that were to happen and you had an insurance agent on your team, they could tell you, "This person had a significant amount of damage to their house from hail." Then we could step in, send a direct mail piece to that person and let them know we're interested, that we saw they have hail damage to their property.

Or, you could give them a call and say, "Hi, I was referred to give you a call from so and so, and they wanted me to reach out because you recently were involved in one of the big storms that came through. I understand you have a lot of hail damage, and so I wanted to talk to you because I'm a real estate investor. I'm interested in properties like yours. And if you're interested in moving, and not worrying about the repairs, I'm interested in purchasing the property." Most people who have sustained a significant amount of damage to their property, want to move. And that is completely normal.

When we're talking with homeowners, we need to find out balances for mortgages. Is anything else borrowed against the property? Are the taxes current? Are there any judgments? Are there any collections? We want to look for anything that can go against the title. So, that's why an investor-friendly title company is a crucial relationship for you to have. They can check title for you, give you the feedback you need to do your due diligence properly, and put offers in on the properties.

Insurance agents can also handle two other areas that you may encounter when dealing with homeowners. A majority of homeowners don't want to stay in the home anymore when there is fire and mold damage. Let's talk about fire damage. When a fire does happen in the interior of the home, it typically affects the kitchen. It might start in a bathroom if there was some sort of electrical malfunction, a plug left in the outlet that sparked and caught on fire, perhaps.

But most fires happen within the kitchen. Maybe the oven was left on when a roast was inside, that someone forgot about. Once the fire department shows up and puts the fire out, what's left is a very grim sight. So, the homeowner doesn't want to hassle with the contractor and getting everything back to standards when they get the insurance money. That's when people move. From what I've seen, 80 percent of the time, people want to move.

The insurance agent will know exactly what they want to do with the property, because they're going to ask the homeowners questions about keeping the policy. "What do you want to do with the insurance check? Are you wanting to repair the home?" A good insurance agent will follow-up on fire or mold damage problems with the property, because they want to retain the business, even if the policy holder moves. If their client only moves a couple of miles away, the insurance agent can still help them out.

It's imperative that an insurance agent has a good follow-up system and makes sure the homeowner is well taken care of. They have to be thorough when inspecting the fire damage. If the kitchen is completely destroyed, they need to know if it should be replaced entirely and if the drywall needs to come off. They'll have to determine if the studs and the sub-flooring are okay, because sometimes you do have to repair the studs and the sub-flooring.

As long as you're plugging your numbers in with what I like to call your Maximum Allowable Offer, you will want to plug in the right discounted prices. Fire damaged properties can be picked up at bargain costs, depending on the fire damage. You can always talk to the homeowner and let them know you're interested in purchasing the property, so they don't have to worry about doing any of the repairs on the home.

When you tell them your intentions, it will set their mind at ease because they just received an insurance check and are about to get an order to purchase the property. If there is a balance on the mortgage, they could apply that money toward the mortgage. It would be in our favor to purchase the property at a steep discount then. Most of the times, investors don't go after fire damaged properties because they don't know the extent of the structural damage on the property.

As long as you have a trustworthy and capable contractor you can send them over to the fire-damaged, and that contractor could come assess, "We're going to have to rip apart this wall and check the sub-flooring. We're going to have to make sure the beams below this floor are fine." Whether you have a block or a crawl space, you have to check the beams underneath the floor to make sure they are structurally sound and that no one will fall through.

Depending on the scope of damage, you might have to replace some of the roof, if the fire reached a height to damage it. Most of the time, fire damaged houses suffer interior damage.

But sometimes a fire-damaged property will have a fire that starts in the interior and then works its way to the exterior of the home. If that happens, we have to consider siding and other elements of the property, whatever's been affected, that the homeowner does not want to contend with. If you are in this situation, it's a win-win for everybody involved. The insurance agent can serve their client and make them a lot happier since they can move on from the property. The client doesn't have to suffer the headache of rebuilding their property, and the agent can retain the relationship with their client and help them out in their next move.

Once we do the home remodel, or wholesale, or rehab the property, whatever we want to do, it's important that we push the next person who purchases to accept it as their final destination. This means we want to sell it to either a first-time home buyer, or a family. When I say, "final destination," I just mean we're done with the property. It's rehabbed. It's move-in ready.

We can tell the new owner, "The insurance agent completely helped us out. They're phenomenal. They're great to work with and are going to get you the lowest possible price on insuring the property. If you want to use them, they are one of the best in the area." This is a relationship-building opportunity for you to establish continuing business every month arising from fire-damaged properties.

If we're talking about mold damage, we're on a different level. Like fire, you have to come into mold properties with a mask, so you don't breathe in anything harmful. Many people don't even realize mold is growing in their homes, especially in the Midwest, because the climate is drier. When we deal in other states like Florida, that have high humidity. mold is a common occurrence that is actually visible on the exterior of a lot of properties.

When mold is green, in that stage, it is easy to spray off. Sometimes owners may have a rental or a vacant property that's been empty for an extended period. Say, for instance, the power goes out, and then rain comes in and floods the basement. When that happens, the water might sit there without anyone even knowing.

If it's 75, 80, 85 degrees outside, then mold will grow. Without proper ventilation, and adequate airflow, mold will grow. Once mold forms, especially on carpet and drywall, it seeps through the drywall to the studs. If the mold is unnoticed and untreated for a long time, it turns into a very hazardous black mold. If you inhale black mold, it is so dangerous that people have died. I know that's a harsh way to talk about this danger, but it is reality.

If you get mold spores in your lungs, it's a critical situation. That's why, when it comes to mold, you MUST wear masks whenever you're going through damaged properties. Having the proper support over your nose and mouth is very, very crucial. When homeowners see what's happened to their property, they may not be interested in repairing it, depending on the severity of damage. Most of the time, mold appears in basements, but it could also affect main floors in properties without basements.

Mold happens to properties, regardless of whether they are occupied or not. If it goes untreated and you can't see it, people will start getting sick. Sometimes, they'll wonder why, and it's because of mold. Mold must be properly treated by somebody who's licensed, insured, and bonded. Most of the time, they come in, rip off all the drywall in the basement and spray everything with their chemicals to treat and destroy the mold. These experts use materials that they can completely disinfect from any future mold growth, and that will also take care of the existing mold growth.

Since checks have to be cut from the insurance company, guess who's going to be the first one to tell you about the property? The insurance agent. The insurance agent will reach out to you, to let you know: "We've got some properties with mold. The owner does not want to keep them, and I'm letting you know because, I told the owner that you buy mold properties, and they're very interested in talking to you."

A good investor-friendly insurance agent will talk to the owner to determine if they want to sell, and if they do, the best action the insurance agent can take is to refer that individual to you. Your agent can tell the owner: "If you're interested in selling, we do know a real estate investor. I've worked with him many times. He can come in, help you out and take the property completely off your hands, so you don't have to worry about the mold. They have the right type of mold remediation company that comes through your home, takes care of it, and then they'll end up fixing up the property, and selling it to another homeowner. As a real estate investor, they do many of these deals."

Mold works the same as fire. As soon as the insurance agent talks to the owner about setting up a plan to reimburse them for the repairs, through a claim for reimbursement, the ball starts rolling. An insurance agent will notify you about other property opportunities as well, including vandalism and burglary. When these events happen, property owners may experience post-traumatic stress.

This situation can hit a newer family hard, especially if they have small children. If the house is broken into, they could get a little freaked out, and depending on the damage, it could be very stressful for the family. They may choose to move, even though the house might be in a good area. Because maybe the crime was such a shock to the system that they just want to get out. Again, the homeowner will contact the insurance agent, put in the claim, and then they will want everything completely remedied. If they want to sell, it's another opportunity for us to come in, relieve them of their situation, and purchase the property.

Your insurance agent should be investor-friendly, and to find them you can do the same thing you did to find your investor-friendly real estate agent: look on Zillow and Craigslist. You can also take a few minutes and do two searches. Search Google and type in your area. If I wanted to find an insurance agent in my town, I would type in, "Indianapolis Insurance Agent." When you do this for your location, a bunch of results will pop up. You can also look on YouTube, too to find more agents to work with on your properties.

On YouTube, type in "Insurance Agent in Indianapolis," or, "Indianapolis Insurance Agent," and you will find their videos. Locate a person who actively posts videos and who uses Facebook regularly. It's a smart idea to also work with someone who's hungry. They've likely got a good book of business, and you are ready to help them out as they help you. It's a two-way street, a give and take relationship. But that's how all long-term relationships last, by entering into an arrangement where you give business, and they take business, and then vice versa.

In conclusion, you need to go out, find insurance agents to work with immediately, who can help to transform your business, and then you will start to receive three, four, and five potential lead opportunities every month. If your insurance agent is doing their job, and they've got a solid book of business, you're going to get notifications of discounted properties quite frequently. When you find your investor-friendly insurance agents, you'll see results happen within your business from an entirely different revenue opportunity.

Chapter 6: YouTube's Flipping Relationship Builder

"Go for it now. The future is promised to no one." - Wayne Dyer

YouTube is an effective site for finding new buyers and sellers. But, for the particular instance we'll talk about, I want to show you a relationship builder within YouTube that will allow you to use it at a pace to see results within a quick period. On YouTube, the search engine box allows me to type in practically whatever I want. Say, for instance, I type in "real estate Indiana." The search engine will pull up all the channels or videos for Indiana. That's a lot of results to wade through, so I'm going to use the filter button that permits me to sort by upload date, type, duration, and features.

Then I'll go to "Type" and click on "Channel." I want to find the types of channels featuring active real estate investors. The more active they are, the sweeter it is for me. There are several different findings that will be returned to you. You can search using various keywords to locate several different channels on YouTube. The beautiful effect is once you see the information coming in, you can go to all the channels and start contacting the folks behind them.

When I typed in "real estate Indiana," and set up my filter, I picked up numerous channels. The first one that pops up is Indiana Real Estate Investments. If I click on them, I see there's not a whole lot of information. Their channel has the subscriber count, but it's not a high amount. They only have one video, but they've subscribed to other places. I probably don't want to do anything with them, so I will hop back out, and see if there are any other channels that might be a better fit to help me.

We didn't get a ton of channels back, so we'll enter titles in the search engine box. "We Buy Houses," for instance. Whenever you type in "We Buy Houses," YouTube will pull up a tremendous number of individuals. You want to narrow down your choice to a specific city; if I wanted to find results in Indianapolis, I'd click on "Indianapolis." So, "We Buy Houses Indianapolis" is what it would return. And as soon as I type that keyword in, I can see 8,340 results. That's a decent number for videos. But again, not exactly what I'm trying to find. I'm trying to find, channels through the use of the filter function.

When I use the filter again, then I receive 130 filtered results. Now, let's say I go to the result that says, "We Buy Indianapolis Houses." They've presented a very clear picture of exactly what they do. They have a "Contact Us Today," option listing their phone number. They have 486 subscribers and get a decent amount of views on their videos. It looks like they're doing a lot of business. They've got a Facebook business page, and phone number as well. So, when you take the time to do your research on YouTube, it allows you to find specific people in your area that you can do business with right away. You don't have to wait to get going. You don't have to send out a mailer. You don't have to try to a slew of different things that will hinder your performance and not get you the results you ultimately want. At the end of the day, we want you to see results because without the results, then it will be extremely difficult for you to close transactions and then make money.

After checking out their channel, I want to get in contact with the people at "We Buy Indianapolis Houses." I would give them a call, but before I do that, I want to stress that I don't view these people, or this company, as a competitor. I view them more as an individual or entity to do joint venture transactions with. Most people are already putting the word out; they're sending a direct mailer, maybe paying for pay-per-click ads on Google and Facebook. Maybe they've already set up their relationships with attorneys, title companies, and real estate agents. They might have buyers for their properties. These people can prove to be a great resource for you. You can bring them deals if you want to sell something fast, for instance. It's also a wise idea to get on their list of individuals interested in purchasing properties.

Whenever I help a person get into the real estate investing business, I always recommend they have a buyers' list set up. A lot of these people will be on your list. So, if I go back to my results, I can see 130 channels on YouTube with, "We Buy Houses Indianapolis." This channel might not use the same format as "We Buy Houses," but, "We Buy Indianapolis Houses," are branding themselves correctly. Before you get on the same bandwagon and create your own "We Buy (Your City) Houses," you should know that the "We Buy Houses" is trademarked, and you need to be very, very careful about how you use that phrase, so you don't get sued. I recommend consulting with an attorney.

To get around that legality, you can type in your city between "Buy" and "Houses." In our case, I know the individual owning this channel. I helped to design it and worked with them to grow their subscribers. I can see they also get a decent number of viewers on their videos from their subscribers. As we scroll down, I can see a lot of channels do not have the same kinds of numbers. One channel has 25 subscribers. Another person has 80. We want to do a little better than that. Still, another has 63,000 subscribers, and it looks like they might have a TV show? But I like the data.

You want to find channels and people that have what you need. The site with lots of subscribers is called "Less Junk, More Journey." From a real estate investing standpoint, they might not fit our bill. "We Buy Indianapolis Houses" has a much more inviting feel than "Less Junk, More Journey." So, we're going to go after them. They've got their phone number on their channel. Everything's prevalent; it's listed right there to get in contact with everybody. When we give them a call, the conversation can be uncomplicated and easy. I'm simply stating: "Hello, my name's Jason Lucchesi. I'm giving you a call, in reference to your YouTube channel. I see you have some videos and that your phone number was on there as well. The main reason for my call is I wanted to follow up with you, to see if there's anything we can do together, from doing some deals to getting deals flipped. I do have some buyers lined up right now, so what I'm looking for is deals."

You don't need to use what I wrote verbatim. The best thing you can do is simply call them. Give them a quick buzz, see if you can make a connection. When you get to their channel, go to the "About" section. The "About" section tells you when they joined, how many views their page has (if that's something they want to divulge), and any links. In this particular case, there's a Google+ profile with a few posts associated with their channel. Certainly, scan their Google+ page or whatever link they've listed. If their website is public, click on the link and also head over to their Facebook, Twitter, and Instagram pages, etc.

You want to find out more information about these individuals, so you can have a good quality conversation. Nothing hurts more than making a call without researching information about your prospect. The more prepared you are, the better your conversations. If they're doing walkthroughs of properties with three-bedroom, two baths, and you see there are a lot of those types of properties in your searches, that's an indicator you could provide value to them. When you call them, you can say, "I'm coming across a lot of three-bedroom, two-bath properties. I wanted to see if you were interested in any of those properties. I'd like to know if you guys are interested because I saw some of your videos exploring a lot of three-bedroom, two-bath properties."

After you gather some information, you'll have a strong strategy for diving in deep and talking to YouTube channel owners to see if they would be interested in your properties. Let's examine some other channels. You'll note emails and phone numbers both. I'm looking at the "We Buy Houses for Cash Indianapolis;" they have 10 subscribers and three videos. I'll click on one of them, and I can read it says, "Realtors versus Investors who buy houses for cash." They are using the keywords of buying houses for cash to improve their search engine optimization. Doing this also gets them ranked properly on Google because the search term "Buy Houses" comes up quite a bit. Remember this as you search for just the right channels. A lot of people fail to properly use keywords in the "Description" field of their YouTube video channel.

First and foremost, make sure the URL to your website is listed. It needs to be prominent on YouTube. Then make a paragraph describing your videos or your company. You can use the same content for every single video, but the bigger aim is to make sure you use the right keywords in the description. That's how you will rank higher on YouTube. Let's say you insert a paragraph with four sentences. Each sentence should have your keyword associated with it. Once you end your paragraph, you should list your website again. You can't just put JasonLucchesi.com. You need to use the entire URL: http://www.JasonLucchesi.com. When you do this, it makes your link live so folks will be able to click on it instead of copying and pasting it into the address bar. We want to eliminate those extra couple steps. It makes it easier for people to click through to your site when they look at your YouTube channel. You've given them all the contact information they need to reach you.

I'm assessing a channel right now, and it's not very user-friendly. As soon as I land on it, there's not a clear answer to the question: "How do I reach out?" Or, "How do I email you?" To reach out to these people I had to go to their video where their phone number and their dot-com are listed. But again, they have nothing within the description field. I highly encourage folks to provide their information right away. You should have it available and in front of prospect's eyes as quickly as possible. Cover art is also huge. On a site we built for a client, we ensured it was very user-friendly. So, when I land on their profile, it contains "Contact Us" information, a logo of the company, and the ability to clearly see where the videos are housed. We can take people through the steps they need to complete to reach us.

Logos can be created for five bucks on Fiverr, which is a site that is quite easy to use. Once you're on Fiverr, type in "logos" and search for the person with the best ratings. The same process applies if you want to get somebody to build custom cover art for you. When you're on Fiverr, you can also type in "YouTube cover" to find people doing YouTube covers. It's relatively fast. Whatever artwork you need can be done in about three to five days at most as long as you don't ask for anything too complicated.

You can also use other keywords like, "sell my house." And then enter your city. So, I would enter "sell my house Indianapolis." It pulls up 84,200 videos. When I filter by type and select "Channel," it gives us 219 filtered results. We can see different types of subscriber counts. Again, that's not going to make a major difference. Your goal is to get phone numbers for the people you want to talk to.

When we scroll down, we can see "Spouses Buying Houses," and their URL: spousesbuyinghouses.com. The phone number is listed, and that is so inviting and very friendly. Marketing in this way allows you to reach out to them. Here's another option: "Ben Buys Indie Houses, Trusted Indianapolis Home Buyers." They don't have cover art, so it's hard for me to find a way to get ahold of these people. I'll probably have to click on his videos and look for contact information. If I go to "Spouses Buying Houses," they do have cover art, but they've missed the point. They've provided no phone number, no email, and no website. If I click on "About," it does note their website. But they forgot to put the "www" before their URL, so it's not a live link.

You can view the email address, but you'll need to verify you're not a robot. Then click "Submit" to pull up their email: hello@spousesbuyinghouses.com. They've been on YouTube since 2009 and have 12,201 views for their videos posted. They have a decent number of videos but not many views. It's a very low count, within the single digits. You could still give them a call because I don't put a lot of weight into those numbers. These people may not have their online game in check, so you may have to reach out in a different manner and get ahold of them. That's why calling them is still a viable option.

The "sell my house" keyword will yield some promising results, and as we have done before, just add in your city. You could look up "sell your house," instead of "sell my house." We've got 6,300 results from that search, and that's a decent number. I can see 76 channels using that same search on YouTube. If people are using the whole, "We Buy Indianapolis Houses," gig or the "We Buy Chicago Houses," they will more than likely rank similarly as the rest of the keywords we're talking about. It's simple. Start searching and then start reaching out to folks to see if they have deals to partner on. The takeaway is to take advantage of the free opportunity of YouTube. You will find a lot of cash buyers and investors with deals they would like to sell.

You also want to reach out to attorneys or title companies. Enter "real estate attorney" and then your city. So, I typed in "real estate attorney in Indianapolis." I helped my attorney get their videos ranked pretty high, and I can see their video is the first result. My attorney is Mr. Matthew Griffith. We follow the same process for filtering and find the channel, so we can see all the individuals that you would like to start reaching out to, to talk real estate investing. Our search results show 31 attorneys in the Indianapolis area for the keyword, "real estate attorney Indianapolis."

You can find real estate agents as well, so you'd use "realtor Indianapolis." When I do this, it pulls up 14,500 videos. When we sort by channels, our result is 119. If we do the same thing for "real estate agent" and use your city—Indianapolis, in my case—we've got 12,200 videos and 85 channels.

Using YouTube and conducting these specific searches are strategic ways to start building out your team. YouTube has so many different opportunities to grow and expand your business. I highly encourage you to start using it right away because you could start seeing results within your business immediately. You'll have website information, email information, and best of all, a phone number so you can reach out. Not only will you fill your team with experts in their field, but before you know it, you will have deals under contract from a multitude of agreements: joint ventures, funding the deal, buying the deal, and then reselling it, even rehabbing transactions.

Chapter 7: Flipping Craigslist

"Success is not final, failure is not fatal: it is the courage to continue that counts." - Winston Churchill

Craigslist is an untapped market. A lot of people use the site for a lot of different things. We're going to search for currently available properties, and we're also going to use some of the same methods as YouTube. Craigslist allows us to build up our team as well. Now, Craigslist has transformed since I started using it back in 2008. The look of the actual site itself hasn't changed much, but a lot of the functionality is different.

Go to the area on the site called "services." Services will take me to the real estate section. When I click on "real estate," it's going to pull up within my specified Indianapolis area anyone and anybody having anything to do with real estate investing.

I can see 365 results. The first one that pops up says, "We sell investment properties at wholesale prices." The second one is: "We buy houses," and it states, "FS Houses." That means "For sale" houses.

As we scroll down, we're going to find more and more results just like those first two. We'll note houses for sale, perfect for flipping, and cash buyers wanted. We'll sift through wholesale deals and investment properties for sale. Sites like Craigslist allow you to utilize free sources that are literally at your fingertips. If you've got time to search during breaks at work, you can even cruise Craigslist right from your phone. It's extremely easy. Again, there's no excuse for not finding the right types of deals for your business and not forming the right types of relationships that will lead to your success.

"We sell investment properties at wholesale prices" is my pick. It says, "Looking for investment property for your portfolio. We sell houses cheap. Contact us now for more info." Click on the yellow box, and it will have the phone number and email you need.

The email is not going to be a regular Gmail, Yahoo or MSN email service. The person who set up the listing's email is protected by Craigslist. You'll see a generic, randomized email instead. Just copy and paste the Craigslist email and send them off a message. Even better, you can give this particular person a call because their phone number is prevalent in their ad. You can say, "I saw your ad on Craigslist and that you have properties for sale. I'm looking to add to my portfolio (or I'm looking to add rehab or wholesale properties to my buyer's list)."

Always be transparent. Being honest and open will get you to that next level of communication. If you don't conduct your business and yourself with integrity, and ethically, the person is more than likely going to find out and not want to do business with you ever again. I hold myself to the absolute highest standard, and I'm sure you do as well. But just make sure you're fully transparent with the other person in the transaction.

When I'm contacting somebody, I simply say, "Hey, it's Jason Lucchesi. I saw you had an ad on Craigslist and the ad was, 'We sell investment properties at wholesale prices.' One of the things that I'm looking for right now as an investor are properties at wholesale prices, and I'm hoping to make a decision here relatively quickly. I was wondering if you could help me." That's a great way to open a conversation and get movement from the other end of the phone because now your new contact will want to find out a little bit more about you, too.

You will want to find out where they are getting their deals. Say, for instance, you only want to wholesale properties, it's best to have your cash buyers lined up already because if you don't have your cash buyers on tap, you're not going to know exactly what to ask from the real estate investor. What if I called a real estate investor and they told me what they have, and then I got all excited thinking, *oh, man. All of these are going to be great deals. I'm going to be able to do a whole lot. This is just awesome. They've got properties. This is great.* After you get all hyped up, then you'll start getting properties under contract. The next thing you know, you've talked to some individuals about buying your deals, and they're not even interested because the properties are in undesirable areas.

So, just have a simple conversation with your cash buyers before you start making any calls to potential sellers whether we're talking investors, attorneys, title companies, agents, or whomever it may be. Don't contact anybody until you know from your cash buyers or your private money lenders where they want to buy. Because if you talk to a savvy real estate investor and they know the area really well, they may realize, "Man, that area is really not that great." If that happens, you may jeopardize yourself right out of the gate, if you don't find out that relevant information from your people immediately.

A basic question can save you such headaches. "Where are you looking to buy properties right now?" If they're really vague and don't tell you, just reply, "Okay. I just want to make sure I'm not giving you properties you don't want to look at because some properties we do come across may not be in the most desirable areas, but they still have opportunity for profits to be made. That's why I want to find out what type of areas you want to buy in. Where did you buy your last few houses?"

You buyers can even give you ZIP codes. They might have certain townships, cities or counties they like, and when you know this, you can make good decisions when talking to other people. Once you start building up your company, your brand, and your name, then people will want to rely on you. If you're a reliable source for them, your relationship will turn into a solid win-win for you and everybody involved. You will help everybody take their businesses to the next level. When you are transparent, you set the expectation up front and it puts you in the driver's seat throughout the entire transaction.

When you are looking under services for real estate, search for the ads that say, "We buy houses." Another result I'm looking at right now says, "We buy houses," and it has the FS houses listed. This particular ad tells me all the areas where this person is buying properties which is a really useful fact. It helps me out quite a bit because I can find out right away that they are a cash buyer looking for deals in a particular area. That's a winning strategy. We can find out precisely what they want from looking at their Craigslist posting. Then we just need to verify the information, and this will really make them appreciate that you took the time to read their ad. You didn't just give them a random phone call without knowing a lick of what they put in their ad.

In this particular ad, if I go to the yellow box for replying, I can see the phone number and the Craigslist email. So, I can reach out to them and build a foundation for the relationship to come. To establish our firm footing, I want to give them a call as quickly as possible.

Another great way to find deals is to use the main page of Craigslist and look under "housing." This tab is in the middle, and from there you can mouse down to "real estate for sale." Now, when you get to "real estate for sale," you want to bypass all the properties listed with real estate agents. Go to the upper left-hand corner. You'll see housing in the middle and in the last section, "Real estate for sale." Click the little dropdown and then click on "real estate - by owner." In this example, 1,154 properties appeared.

Again, it boils down to what your cash buyers want in wholesaling or rehabbing. If you're seeking rental properties, it's key to know exactly what you want. Craigslist allows you to filter and conduct different searches on properties with different criteria, like a three-bedroom and one-bath minimum. Once I put in those particular parameters, it will give me exactly what I want. If I put in a minimum of three bedrooms and one bathroom, it will return 576 properties.

You can search for properties by square footage. Go to the housing type on the left-side column of Craigslist and select the housing type. In the Midwest, we don't have a large number of real estate investors seeking condos. You want to find single-family properties Check off "house," and the search engine will allow you to sort that way. Your results will reflect what you've filtered.

Here in Indiana, and some other Midwestern states, townhouses can move pretty quickly. If I click to update the search for "house" and "townhouse," my results don't change much. Now. I'm looking at 495 houses. That's still a big list of homes for sale. You want to go through and look at each individual listing. I have my view set in gallery format, so I can view properties on a grid. Here's a flip handyman special, four bedrooms, two and a half baths and it's on an acre.

Once I click on it, it's going to tell me more. The ad says, "All this house needs is a little TLC. This home sits on a one-acre wooded lot. There's no homeowner's association in the neighborhood. It's a quiet street. The home is a four-bedroom, two and a half baths with a spare den or playroom as well. If a closet is added, it could be a fifth bedroom, or knock out the wall and open up the kitchen. Roof is less than five years old. Flip the home for a profit or keep and make great cash flow."

This property is listed for 99,000, and they've also included in the ad that the home next door sold for $228,000. When you call these folks, find out as much information as possible. If you're wholesaling, you want to look at the property. They've added quite a few pictures. As I'm looking at these pictures, one of the rooms has a lot of writing on the wall. It's graffiti, and a certain type of marker was used. It may look to an inexperienced investor like black mold, but I think somebody just let their kid go all out on this room with marker. The rest of the house is appealing. The flooring looks in great shape. The drywall looks fine, but it needs paint. It looks really promising, although the tile in the kitchen is outdated.

I appreciate they've noted the roof isn't that old. The owner probably just up and left, and they might be in a very distressed position. The bathroom looks okay, very dated. You'll find that a lot of these properties are going to be extremely dated. Those are prime properties. You want to find properties in a distressed state because those are the deals that will be priced at a substantial discount. You might find deals from asset managers, or hedge funds and attorneys who may have probate or divorce opportunities. However these properties came onto the market, let me stress the distressed properties are the gems we're trying to find.

We have pictures of the actual master bedroom here. The carpets are completely destroyed. The doors are going to need work. We'd have to clean up the outside of the property because curb appeal sells. Make sure you go in knowing exactly what's going to be needed and do a video of the entire property as well as take pictures.

In the yellow box to get in touch, this person has left their name and number which is advantageous because we love saving money and using free resources. I can call this number right away. I don't have to wait days on end to hear back either because they also left their email.

I would say the following. "Hello, my name is Jason Lucchesi. I saw your ad on Craigslist for the property that you have listed at $99,000. It looks like it's a four-bedroom. We're real estate investors, and these are the types of properties we're looking for. Do you have a second to tell me a little bit more about this home?"

You want to let them know where you found their information because once you've disclosed that, it makes it so much easier for you to proceed and allows their guard to drop a little bit. It's not going to be down completely because you still need to work on the relationship. The best way to do this is by asking questions about the property. Who is the person listing the property? Is it the actual homeowner or is it another investor wanting to wholesale it? You never know until you ask questions. And you can start gathering those facts ASAP when you give them a phone call.

Just do the simple search we discussed, and you could start finding properties that are fix and flippers, properties that need TLC, properties that are in a very distressed state. You can also conduct these searches virtually and from anywhere in the world. You can find properties and get them under contract faster than you realize. As long as you have the right types of buyers on your list, it will be pretty seamless to sell the properties and close 100 percent of them.

Chapter 8: Why Do I Need a Flipping Attorney?

"The price of success is hard work, dedication to the job at hand, and the determination that whether we win or lose, we have applied the best of ourselves to the task at hand."
- Vince Lombardi

As a real estate investor, I learned when I started in 2008, that it is extremely important to network with the right people. Shortly before I became an investor, I was living on unemployment checks and didn't know exactly what to do to find deals and buyers. But I knew I could go out and at least begin networking with the right people. One of the very first people I started connecting with outside of a real estate agent and title company, was an attorney.

Attorneys handle a lot of different jobs besides going to court all day long. They deal with divorces, bankruptcies, probates, and foreclosures. They handle negotiations for short sales, evictions for landlords and any type of property loss due to damage from either fire, tornado, or hurricane. They work with insurance agents on those property losses as well. Their clients are people that we, as real estate investors, can help.

When I became a real estate investor and wanted to make it my full-time career, I surrounded myself with the right people. The right people include real estate agents, title companies, attorneys, wholesalers, and the wholesalers you can do JV deals with. As a beginner, you need to account for those four. Number five on your team could be a general contractor you can use for repair quotes. You can send them to your cash buyers, but that's optional. You don't need a general contractor when you are getting your feet under you, but it does help.

There are several benefits to working with an investor-friendly attorney. When you talk to the attorney, tell them you're a real estate investor, and that you can close on transactions very quickly. If you don't have a track record that is completely fine. It's best to meet with your attorney face-to-face, for a chat. Let them know what you want to do, either wholesaling or rehabbing, the buy and hold side. Being completely clear and transparent is key to your integrity. Let them know your intentions.

Say, for instance, an executor of an estate, (in the case of probate cases), approaches this attorney. They let them know they don't want the property anymore. More than likely the attorney is going to urge the executor to do their own due diligence and hire a real estate agent or an auction company. Imagine if you were the person to get the referral on that property. If you close a wholesale deal with an A to B, B to C transaction, it will get you more than just a foot in the door with the attorney. It puts you in the seat right across from the attorney positioning you for a plethora of leads consistently month after month.

When we're talking about dealing with divorces, bankruptcies, probates, foreclosures, short sales and evictions, most of the time someone will need to sell the property because the other individual, the spouse or significant other, doesn't have enough money to pay the mortgage. Maybe the house is too big for one person, so they end up selling it and putting the money into the settlement, so they can part properly after selling their property.

One of the best positions you can take is to be someone who solves a particular problem, or a huge obstacle for many people. Most of the time attorneys don't know how to solve these issues quickly, and a lot of these dealings need to be executed in a timely manner. If a real estate agent takes over, the property may sit for a certain period of time, but if you're a referral from an investor-friendly attorney, the situation could develop to determine what the parties will take and what the best offer will be.

When we talk to people in a distressed state from various life circumstances such as divorce, it's very stressful. People just want to move on most of the time. They want to part ways as quickly as possible; rip the cord and be done with it. If the house is valued at $180,000, for instance, they might have a mortgage for $80,000. You can come in, make an offer for 100,000. As long as you're paying off the mortgage, and both parties are getting some cash, it's a win-win. Is it going to work out exactly the way I've just explained it? Well, you won't wrap up these situations like that every time, but it will happen consistently as long as you keep talking to enough people.

The same situation applies to folks facing bankruptcy. Depending on the type of bankruptcy that they're going to be filing, either a chapter 7 or 13, if it's a 7, the debt will go back into the bankruptcy. Sometimes, the house may return to the mortgage company. But, if you can come in before the person or couple decides to file for bankruptcy, depending on if there's equity in the house, you could make a decent offer on the property that allows the party to not put the house in the bankruptcy. If the house winds up in the bankruptcy, then a deed in lieu will have to be filed. A bankruptcy and a deed in lieu on an individual's credit is going to destroy it for the next seven years.

Instead, you could buy the house, then pay off the mortgage, and doing so will help that person in a financial pickle exponentially because, even though they will still have to contend with the bankruptcy, at least their property wasn't foreclosed. That's the last delinquent item they need on their credit to get their lives back on track. Once you file bankruptcy, your credit score dives, and it stays at that level for years, but if you can ensure their mortgage is not affected, it serves your client well.

Sometimes, you will find properties before they enter into bankruptcy, and when that happens, you can get them at a substantial discount. Once they've been included, it's extremely hard to get approved as that has to go through a trustee, and once it's approved by the trustee it's then subject to approval by bankruptcy court. You'll have to deal with many different roadblocks, and it becomes a painful situation that is dragged out over time.

As it pertains to foreclosures, we will, obviously, want to be notified right away when there's a foreclosure because, typically, a bank will hire a real estate agent, and they will list the property. An attorney and their firm are going to be hired by the bank to take care of the legal details. That's why, if you can get in good with an investor-friendly attorney who has relationships with banks, it is to your benefit. For example, if your attorney receives the note of a property they need to sell, the mortgage company or bank will want to get rid of it as quickly as possible. If they can bypass having to list it and paying a real estate agent, they would rather sell the property to you.

You can get deals before they hit the market because a lot of individuals will want to sell the properties off-market. Imagine if you can get an REO before it hits the MLS. Your deals will be sold quickly because you've avoided putting them on the open market, or any site be it MLS, Craigslist, Zillow, etc. It's an optimal time for you to take advantage and get the REO, then rapidly wholesale it.

Now, let's talk short sales. A short sale happens when the property is negotiated for a lower rate. Let's say, the house is worth $150,000, and the mortgage is $200,000. We want to negotiate the current balance of $200,000 to, $75,000. An attorney will handle the negotiations. As of the writing of this book, a lot of attorneys are starting to handle negotiations with banks because they can expedite the process far faster than investors or even real estate agents. But we can be the buyer on those properties. If your attorney says, " I've got three properties that my clients can't make the payment on anymore. They owe more than what the house is actually worth and just want to get out of the properties," you can help them and make money doing it.

Now, instead of having the owners do a deed in lieu, which basically means they sign the house back over, ruining their credit in the process, you can inform the attorney, "I'll put offers on those properties. Why don't we try and negotiate a short sale?" If you're doing a short sale and you negotiate it correctly, when you close, it will show up on the credit as an account that has been settled for less than what's owed. It'll ding the credit, but at least that person will know they can start to rehab their credit within the next six to 12 months.

Short sales allow you to pick up properties at substantial discounts. It's not unheard of for a property to go for $150,000, when the actual mortgage is $200,000. When that happens, the bank wants to get rid of the property quickly because it shows on their books as a negative balance. If the FDIC audits them, they can be fined. Think about it, if you're a bank and your balance sheet is in the red from having too many mortgages worth more than what the property is, you'll want to liquidate those properties yesterday.

You can even help with landlord evictions. You're in a prime position to let your attorney know if they're filing evictions, you'd like to know because some landlords might be a bit strapped and want to sell. You can come in and make offers on the properties the owner is leasing out or renting and that they just want to get rid of. It does happen often.

Most of the time the landlords own multiple properties, and that could be a really great situation for you. You might even get a package deal if you can negotiate at the right price. You can even move an entire package to one buyer. That's why it's really important to know the cash buyers on your list. You will be aware if they are looking for multiple properties. If these properties have problematic tenants, it might be a matter of getting the right property manager appointed to take care of the issues.

Property loss will be mainly handled through your insurance company. We discussed that in a previous chapter, and if you need a little more insight, I highly encourage you to go back to that specific chapter to learn about how the insurance agent and attorney can work synergistically. Again, if the attorney receives notice of this information, the insurance rep is going to receive this type of information, too. If you don't have an insurance agent on your team, but the attorney does, then you can find out who that insurance company is, and who the representative is. Once you do, you can work with that contact, too.

If you're closing deals with your attorney, a lot of times the attorney is going to want to get involved in your transactions. They may be extremely busy, so they would appreciate your telling them about opportunities. If they see you wholesaling and making good money you can explain to them, "If you lent money on this particular transaction we would make exponentially more money." People want to make money. They might have money in the stock market. They might have money in money market accounts, or retirement accounts that aren't making them anything. Give them, 8-9 percent on their money for lending it to you for transactions, and you can level up from making $10,000 to $15,000 as a wholesaler to $40,000 to $50,000. If that is your scenario, they will do that all day long with you.

You attorney is more than just a referral source. You can talk to them and see if they might be interested in providing private money, or if they know someone who would be interested. They're in contact with a lot of clients, and some of them could be very high-net-worth individuals looking to place their capital. Attorneys also recommend financial advisors to their clients. You can get into that network and start to work with multiple people to get more private money lined up. Private money is huge, and one of your pipelines could come from your investor-friendly attorney.

You may have to talk to quite a few people to find the right members for your team. Because some people may not be on board with what you want to do. When you find this out, it only means they are not a fit for you and your business. Try these four resources to locate your most valuable people: Google, YouTube, Facebook and LinkedIn.

On Google, do a simple search and type in your city, and enter "attorney." For example, I would use "Indianapolis attorney." Then go down the list. You'll see websites and

YouTube videos. You're probably going to have to talk to 20 to 25 attorneys to find the right one. Remember, they must be investor-friendly. You might even find good attorneys at your local real estate investor associations.

If you use YouTube, type in "your city attorney." For example, type in "Indianapolis attorney." The results that come back will likely feature attorneys looking to get more exposure, which means they will more than likely have an open mind to working with you as a real estate investor. You can find their personal profiles on Facebook and go through groups to find these people. They are probably in the real estate related groups. You can also search for them using geographical criteria. In a later chapter, we are going to take a deep dive into using Facebook information to your advantage, so definitely stay tuned.

LinkedIn is another resource. Type in "real estate attorney," or "attorney," and LinkedIn will allow you to put in the locations you want to find your exact types of attorneys.

Our team loves using Google, YouTube, Facebook and LinkedIn, and we enjoy going to real estate investor associations as well. All you need to do is put together the right plan, follow it, and you will start to receive deals from attorneys. You can work with multiple attorneys Just ensure if they're giving you tons of business, you reciprocate in some way.

If somebody needs to talk to an attorney about divorce, bankruptcy, or maybe they've lost a loved one, make sure you give your attorney's name to them. Reciprocal referrals will help you out quite a bit. The attorney gets business, you get business, and the attorney can make money by lending their money to be used as private money in your deals. One of the first actions you need to take when you get into real estate investing is to find an investor-friendly attorney to welcome onto your team immediately.

Chapter 9: Leveraging Flipping Facebook

"The most effective way to do it, is to do it." - Amelia Earhart

One of the biggest opportunities of the 21st century is technology. Technology has busted onto the scene. Right around 2007-2008, Facebook and YouTube received recognition, and Instagram and Twitter followed suit. Suddenly these social media networking platforms were available to all people.

But a lot of people didn't foresee the opportunity to network with Facebook. Facebook goes beyond seeing posts from people checking into the gym or what they had for dessert. It goes so much further. Facebook could be an entire blanket opportunity for you to network with the right individuals.

Say I want to connect with buyers who want to buy the deals I have under contract, or that I'm looking for sellers seeking to sell their property. The cool thing about Facebook is that you will get in with people instantly. You don't have to send out postcards, text messages, or use any other marketing tactics that take time. But there's nothing wrong with those sources. I fully believe direct mail is a huge opportunity. If you have the marketing budget for it, you will see leaps and bounds of growth within your business. Right now, let's discuss how Facebook can provide many opportunities.

The Facebook opportunity allows you to meet the right people and interact with the right groups. On Facebook, go into the search engine field; this is the box you will see toward the top, left-hand corner of the page. Here, you can search for groups. If I type in "real estate" and then click on the little magnifying glass, I'll see all kinds of results: "posts," "people," "photos," "videos," "pages," "places," "groups," "apps," "events," and "links."

We're going into groups, so we need to click on "groups." Once we do, all the different groups will appear. Now, check the filter results. You can select "show only," or "membership." I go to the default section, which is any group pertaining to "show only" and "membership." Now, I can see all the different groups spread out on Facebook.

A lot of these groups require you to join. It doesn't cost you anything. You can join as many groups as you want. LinkedIn has a max of 100 groups to join. Facebook doesn't have a cap.

Next, I'll review all the different groups. For example, the Real Estate Investors Group, has 42,000 members. They average about 10+ posts per day, and all I need to do is click "join." When you click to join the groups, some might ask different questions. This group asks if we are a realtor, investor, or if we provide service for the real estate industry. Let's type in "real estate investor." Groups ask these questions, so they can avoid spammers. If you have too many spammers in the group, it will inhibit the group's growth. Members will constantly see spam ads from people with nothing better to do than post about sunglasses for 90 percent off that are going to break as soon as you put them on your face.

Many group admins are wising up in terms of running a proper group on Facebook. Say I want to go to Metro Detroit Real Estate Investors Group. This group has 2,878 members. When you are searching, narrow down your filters to find groups specifically geo-located in your areas of interest.

If I lived in Detroit, I would want to join the Metro Detroit Real Estate Investors Group; I'd want to start attacking like a bulldog. Seriously, I would take my involvement to a manic level. When we check out the member's section, you'll see all 2,878 members, and you can find out who the admins are. Learn about the different members and start connecting with them.

You will also see who's in your area, and who's already a connection. The settings show you current friends. You'll note members with things in common and members living within your city and state. I want you to look at the people who have recently joined. These are the people who are active on Facebook, and you want to go after them because if you choose to contact people who had initially joined in 2011, they may no longer be active on Facebook. Why would we want to connect with people who are no longer active?

Go to the first person who recently joined, and we'll open them up in a new tab. Then, you'll start looking at their posts. You want to see their timeline for making posts. If they don't have posts that have been recently added to their profile, then you probably don't want to connect with them. If the person hasn't posted within the last two to three weeks, stay away from them, because you won't get your desired results. People who you connect with will either have deals for you or potential buyers for you. If the person you select hasn't posted in a while, then go back to the group and look at the next person down.

If you find a lot of people within your area, that's great for you because you won't have to go through the recently joined. You can, instead, look at the people who recently joined within your area. When you find members within your area go after them and start connecting.

As an example, this woman I'm assessing, has posted within the last 72 hours. So, I know I want to reach out to her. She's in the group we want, so those are two positives. We want to confirm she is an actual real estate investor, so you can click on the dropdown box on her profile where it says "more." The dropdown box contains several options. The first one "videos," then "check-ins" then "groups," and the last one is "notes." We want to go into groups and find all the groups this person is in.

Upon the first check, she looks like she is involved in a lot of different real estate-related groups. This leads me to believe she's active and wants to pursue real estate investing, or she is a current real estate investor. I am going to send this person the following message: "Hi, Debbie. My name is

Jason Lucchesi, and I see we are members of the same group here on Facebook called Metro Detroit Real Estate."

When I mention the group, it gives her a point of contact, so she doesn't have a wall up and she won't be asking herself, *why is this person randomly reaching out to me*? My message continues: "I'm looking to connect with other like-minded real estate professionals that I can do business with." The message is short, simple, and right to the point, so it will allow us to connect with one another. Then I'll close the conversation, "Talk soon, and I look forward to us connecting. Jason."

Because of the research I've done, I can get past the barrier. When you send your message, since you are not friends, it will go into their "other" folder. It will not hit their inbox instantly. I always advise that you send a message first before sending a friend request. Once you start connecting back and forth, your relationship will be solid. At that point, you can send them a friend request and then all your messages will be delivered straight to their inbox.

But, even if you are not friends, once your contact receives your message and clicks accept, you'll also go right into the inbox. If you're maxed out at the 5,000 friends limit, that's not a problem. You can still send the message. Most people do see the messages in the other folder, and as long as you include the right type of message, you'll soon be ushered into their inbox.

It's smart to connect with people who you have a mutual connection with. Because if they see that you have 300+ mutual friends, they'll assume, *well, I'm friends with Dave, and it looks like they're friends with Dave, too. Let me see what this message is all about.*

Using mutual connections is an icebreaker. If you don't have mutual connections, then ensure your message will be well-received and that you're not coming across as too salesy. You wouldn't want to say, "Hey, I've got this tremendous offer. I would love for you to be involved with it." Don't start off your relationship that way. Start it off on a positive foot, so they will understand the relationship is going to be of mutual interest to doing business. When you follow through in this way, the person will want to connect with you; they will want to find out more about you, and you, in turn, can find out more about them.

Let's return to the search function on Facebook for a minute and click on the magnifying glass. As soon as I click on the magnifying glass, I'm looking for pages. I'll see people who have business pages, and I can connect with them. Now, it might be a little more difficult for your message to reach a person who has a lot of likes and followers, and that's why you must have a value proposition that you can bring to the table. When you inform them of all the value they will enjoy, and you make easy for them to respond to you, they will be more apt to want to collaborate.

If you have two or three off-market deals and they're at a deep discount, getting ahold of somebody via their page will be easier. Now, let's click on people with "real estate" within their title, I still want to click on their name, and that will take me right to their profile. Once I'm there, I can see the last time they posted. Again, we want to stay within that two to three-week period. I'm also going to click on "more."

Some people may not allow you to see all the groups they are associated with due to privacy. If that's the case, I wouldn't want to connect with them because I don't think they're the type of person I want on my team. So, I'll stick to looking at people, pages, and groups. The main things that you want to take away from this is sending off a message–that's going to be well received–to people who hold various positions such as real estate attorneys, real estate agents, joint venture partners, and private sellers. You can easily create your team by using this particular method. All you have to do is a little bit of leg work. If you are stretched for time, you can also outsource these tasks to a virtual assistant. Upwork.com introduces you to virtual assistants. Let them know exactly what you're looking for, and then you will meet the people who are a fit for your expectations.

You need a solid network of people that you can rely on to do business with. If you have a smoking hot deal, the last thing you want is *not* to have cash buyers in place. Most of the people you'll meet through Facebook groups will be other real estate investors with cash buyers, or they will have other deals for you. Start building up your cash buyers list by venturing through the real estate groups on Facebook. When you follow this advice, it's a major game changer for you, and as a bonus, it's 100 percent free. Leverage your connections through Facebook groups, and you will see the results you want.

Chapter 10: Flipping Over County Auctions

"Don't wait to be successful at some future point. Have a successful relationship with the present moment and be fully present in whatever you are doing. That is success." - Eckhart Tolle

So many strategies exist for finding deals, but regardless of the structure of your contract, you need to know how much you have picked the properties up for. In other words, this is the make or break profit amount for each property you flip. The discount of how much you could purchase the property for will weigh heavily on whether you get the deal. In this chapter, we will be talking about county auctions and what you must know to realize your maximum profit.

The county auction lists their properties on their website, and a lot of people are discouraged from going to the auctions because the assumption is that they need a certain amount of money lined up before they can even attend. Because of this mindset, you eliminate other real estate investors from competing because they have the pre-conceived notion they need a cashier's check at the ready. In actuality, if you don't have cash, but you do have cash buyers, and you're going on their behalf you're golden. Let's imagine we have a real estate investor in California, and you're purchasing properties in Indiana. The investor will be unable to come to these auctions so somebody like you can go to the auctions and secure deals for them at a substantial discount. Not only will your attendance save them time, it will also give them a great deal. You will earn money as you help another person out.

You can make from 10 to 20 grand, or whatever amount you put on top of the transaction, to create a phenomenal deal for your end real estate investor. A lot of real estate investors also don't know that another person can bid on their behalf, and that can hinder them from taking advantage of the auctions in your local counties. Keep in mind, if you live in a rural area it will be more challenging to attend the auctions, so I recommend you go to those auctions in a larger metropolitan area. Normally the auctions are once a month, and we'll cover more on the timing in a moment.

You can pick up properties auctioned off by a bank. If someone is delinquent on their taxes, you can pick up their taxes through their tax sale. They'll have two separate auctions. One for actual property. And another one for the taxes. You can acquire two types of purchases when this is the case. If you want to get involved with the actual auction property aspect, the bidding is pretty simple. You register yourself. Once bidding starts, it's just like what you see in the movies with the auctioneer at the front, talking 20 miles a minute.

For the most part, it's a pretty fast process. You get your number. You put your number up if you want to make a bid on a particular property. It's a simple one-two. Once you win the property, it would be best to have funds from your end buyer be sent immediately so you can lock up the deal. Since you've structured the deal to receive a fee for your transaction, you need to make sure you get paid. Or if you've done an A to B, B to C transaction using an escrow agreement, and the escrow agreement outlines the funds for your first transaction that you'll be buying from the auction, and that will be secured by your end buyer, this is the time to execute that agreement. You can receive that agreement from your title company, or if you would like one from us, just send us an email to support@jasonlucchesi.com. We're more than happy to send you the Indiana escrow agreement.

If you want to find out what properties are currently available within your county go to your local county website. You can also learn about bidding if you desire. Each state will have their own official website. Within that site will be several different branches of counties. I'll walk you through Marion County, Indiana. When I go to the Indiana website, it's indiana.gov. Regardless of where you are looking in the United States, each county site will be similar and allow you to locate the properties currently for sale and up for auction. You will follow the same process to find tax deeds as well.

On your county website, go to the local government tab. Then click on county. That should bring up another drop-down menu of information. Find "Sheriff" and then click to find the sheriff sales. The sheriff does all the auctioning for property and for deeds, including the tax sale deeds and real estate property. Next, click on "Public Services" to bring up the next tab: "Real Estate Sales."

Now, you can see all the listings of available real estate, and sometimes you can even bid online. View everything within your specific county, but also familiarize yourself with other facets of the bidding process. Look at the sheriff's deed form, the notice of sheriff sales form and the sheriff bid form.

Check out these forms because to look at the properties, you are required to fill them out. It's free. It does not cost you anything to go to the county auction and take a look.

Once you get into the real estate sales, research the real estate sales dates to give you the information you need. You'll see information for the foreclosing attorneys and information on the buyers. In Marion County, auctions are held on the third Thursday of every month. If you don't have cash buyers yet and you just want to check out the auction, I highly encourage you to do so. You need to be comfortable will all parts of the process. In a larger metropolitan area, you'll run into folks like yourself, but you'll also meet people carrying cash.

Talk to these folks after the auction's done. See if they might be interested in some of the other properties we've outlined in this book. Whether you set up your pipeline to flow from this niche in this chapter, or you decide to pick out another niche in other chapters, you will can gain access to valuable cash buyers. Sometimes, the only time these cash buyers go out is when there's an auction. They go to the auctions; they make their bids. And they either win, or they don't.

When you approach the buyers, I would say, "My name's Jason Lucchesi. I saw you were bidding on some properties, and I just want to let you know that I also come across some off-market properties you may be interested in, that are very similar to the properties you were bidding on. If you could, I would love to reach out to you and let you know when we do have some available inventory, so that you can make a decision on purchasing. When we get these properties, they come in and go out fast, because they're at really great discounts. It's unlike the auctions because these are off-market properties, so nobody else is aware of them."

You don't have to say what I did verbatim, but when you get the conversation flowing, you put your foot in the door with real cash buyers looking to buy properties. Once you get them on the line, do not ask for a proof of funds letter. I know it sounds like a backward recommendation, but fewer people get upset when you don't ask for a proof of funds letter.

Instead, ask for the title company information they are using to close. Let's say the person's name is John. Try saying, "Hey, John. I'm glad we were able to connect with one another. If you can, tell me where are you looking to buy properties because I want to make sure I'm getting the right properties in front of you. I'm going to be sending you properties through email, and you can take a look at them immediately. Let me know pretty quickly if you want to move on any of them. If you could, tell me what county you're looking in and also bedroom, bathroom counts. Does that matter to you? Also, do you have a preference for a title company to use for these transactions?" Craft what you want to say in your own words, making sure to include the major points. Then practice saying it, so you feel comfortable.

The main reason I want to find out the title company they're using is it allows me to call them and find out their last recently-closed transaction. If they can't give you the name of the company they close transactions with, that's not a good sign. If they do give you that information, and when you call, if the person has no idea who you're talking about, that's also not a good sign. It is a good sign when you call, and they know precisely who you're talking about. It's awesome if they say, "We just had a closed transaction like a week ago."

If you're going to auctions and have the cash buyers already lined up, check out the instructions on the website, which are under the same tab as "Real Estate Sales." Under "Real Estate Rules for Bidders," check out the mortgage foreclosure bidder instructions. When you read it, you will know exactly where to purchase and how to get your information in order to bid. Also, explore multiple counties (that's something I recommend and encourage).

You need to know tax sale information and surplus sale information. Surplus sales are the properties the county owns, but that they usually don't want to own, meaning they want to get rid of them as quickly as possible—through auction. Due to the circumstances, they want to let the properties go for the highest and best offer. Surplus sales are not held as often, maybe only once a quarter. They begin in the morning, and you don't want to miss them because these auctions are not as heavily attended as others. It's not like something that you see on the *Storage Wars* TV show.

I urge you to check out whatever is available for auction. It's all public record. You can ask for whatever you want to know and get the information at any point in time. When you're looking for tax sale and surplus sales, check under local government, then county, and then treasurer. You'll read information on available properties, how to do the bidding and anything else you want to know. Under buyers, you can check out the bidder registration and see what tax sales are going on. Just click and read up on any detail you're curious about.

You want to have a cash buyer lined up to help you out if you don't have your own cash. Tax sale and tax deeds can be immensely profitable if you have the know-how and the capital to back them up. You need a lot of funds for these deals because all sales will be final at auction. So, plan on putting 25 percent of the amount of the bid down. The percentage can differ from county to county. Now, most of the auctions either want cash, certified check, cashier's check, or a money order. It is clearly stated where to make the checks out to for your county. They don't want personal checks. They don't want business checks. Those will not be accepted.

Successful bidders are not allowed time to go to the bank to secure funds for their purchase. They're very, very strict on that. You need to take care of the bill then and there. Tax sales can be quite profitable, but you also need to know the redemption period within your specific county because some periods are very long. In that case, you don't want to be caught with that particular deed. The only reason I would want to get involved depends on how much it's paying per month. If the tax sale is for 2,000 bucks, I'm the winner, and I'll get paid X percentage for winning that tax sale from the county.

If I bid and I win at 16 percent, then I would be paid that amount for this tax sale deed. If it gets redeemed at the end period, that money adds up, and it's due to me. If the deal is redeemed, the responsible party will have to pay me the $2,000 plus the percentage I was guaranteed when I bought the deed. If the deal is unredeemed, the property then becomes mine. It depends on the situation. Most of the time, if it's unredeemed, there's no mortgage. If does get redeemed, usually the mortgage company will pay for the taxes to take it out of the auction period. They don't want the house to go to auction because if it doesn't get redeemed by the bank, you could take over the property leaving the mortgage company in a really bad spot.

You can protect yourself when you do your financial due diligence on real estate, surplus, and tax sales. Once you've done that, you can move forward and use these extremely profitable strategies to make a ton of money in a flash.

Chapter 11: Flipping for LinkedIn

"Treat failure as a lesson on how not to approach achieving a goal, and then use that learning to improve your chances of success when you try again. Failure is only the end if you decide to stop." - Richard Branson

One of the very first strategies I found when I didn't have a marketing budget was using a social networking site that not a lot of people are implementing. After reading this chapter, I strongly encourage you to use it, because it offers a wealth of information, for connecting with the right people at the right time. This site that we will cover is unlike a lot of other social networking sites. There's no gym selfies, no pics of gourmet brunches; it's devoid of a lot of the silly nonsense found on Facebook. Sure, we all enjoy doing goofy stuff, but you won't find any of that on this site. LinkedIn is a professional platform comprised of almost 400 million active users and is a goldmine of investing prospects.

Since I joined back in 2009, it's completely changed the way I look at connecting with folks. You no longer have to go out and about, unless you want to. I still love going out networking, getting to know people personally. In my eyes, nothing beats it. When you connect with people on LinkedIn, you might meet up for lunch, or go to a local to-do somebody is having. It's always a good idea to put a face with somebody you've met over the Internet. You can connect and build your relationship in a way that wasn't evident before. Is it necessary? Absolutely not. I've connected with some people on LinkedIn that I've known for years, but I've never met them in-person. Will we ever meet face-to-face? I don't know, but it's not required or necessary.

If you don't like going out and seeing people, LinkedIn offers a sound networking strategy. All you need to do is start connecting with folks. Let's go over how to grow your LinkedIn community. LinkedIn has a search feature, like Google, that you can use to meet people. You can find asset managers, portfolio managers, private equity firms, special assets, loan workout officers, hedge fund managers, real estate investors, realtors, title companies, and attorneys. But there are best practices for searching for these people and positions and contacting them.

If you're looking for an attorney or a title company, they're on LinkedIn. If you don't have your real estate license, and you want to connect with a cool realtor to help you out doing HUD transactions, you can find them on LinkedIn.

For this instance, we'll talk about asset managers. When we search for asset managers on LinkedIn, it pulls up several different tabs. You'll see the following: "People," "Jobs," "Content," "Companies," "Groups," and "Schools." We want to click on "People." Before we continue, I'll briefly explain the asset manager role. An asset manager works at a bank. They could work in hedge funds or focus on private equity.

You can get off-market properties from these sources. A lot of people don't advertise they're selling properties, so you must do the reaching out. When you type in "asset manager," results will show people who work for banks, private equity firms, and hedge fund managers. These people might be asset managers for their own companies as well. We want to look on the right-hand column, where it says, "Filter People By." Click on only the second and third connections, because first connections mean we are already linked to those profiles.

So, you'll click second and third connections, and when you do that your search will narrow. If you were to look for all the asset managers, over 2 million people on LinkedIn have asset manager within their title. We don't want to weed through that many people. So, specifying second and third connection accounts gives us a more reasonable group. My numbers will be a little bit different from yours, because I have a different type of network than you do. I have close to 10,000 people in my network. You might have a new account on LinkedIn, or you may have more connections than me. Either way, this strategy works well, as long as you get active on the site.

I can also head over to locations, on the same side where you just clicked to access second and third connections. If I want to find people in the Chicago area, I'll click on greater Chicago, and it will filter my results again. I'm down to about 37,000 people now, but that's still a lot, and it would take me a while to get through all those LinkedIn connections. Also, you can only search 100 people at a time, so it's imperative that you dial in a number you can handle that will show active users. You can further narrow by selecting people who only speak English; you can select specific companies, too, and type in keywords.

If you want asset manager to be the only title, type in "asset manager" and LinkedIn will provide individuals with "asset manager" in their title. When I did that, I lowered my countdown to 983 results. That's much more manageable. As you skim through these people, you want to find accounts of people you wish to connect with.

First, make sure the person has a profile picture, and that you have a profile picture on your account too. If you don't have a picture, it's time to fix that. Most of us have smartphones; if you don't, find a family member or friend with one and have them snap a photo for you. Then load it up on your LinkedIn account. You have no excuse for not having an actual picture of yourself on LinkedIn. If your prospect doesn't have a picture, go to the next person, because they likely don't have an active account on LinkedIn. Even though there are millions upon millions of people on the site, they may have set up their account just to set it up. Here are a few tips you should look out for when seeking out a potential candidate.

Next, make sure the person has a background image. If they don't have a background image, you'll see the default image LinkedIn posts. Noticing the type of background image is another key factor, I want proof they actually took time to make their profile look good. The background image is not a deal breaker, but I do want to know the effort they expended. Most of them post the skyline of the city where they live. While you're on their profile, check out their URL. You will know if the person took the time to claim their profile if the URL lists LinkedIn.com/in/their name. And since you are already signed into LinkedIn take a moment to claim your profile if you haven't done so already.

My account says either Jason Lucchesi, or Jason C. Lucchesi, after the forward-slash part, but if the person you're vetting is using the default settings from LinkedIn, the URL will have a bunch of numbers and letters, and then their name. We've search-engine-optimized URLs and accounts for clients, so after the forward-slash, depending on their city of residence, we'd put, for example, "we buy Chicago Houses." We do this, so when someone's searching Google, if they're looking for somebody selling or buying houses, their LinkedIn profile will pop up. If you have your phone number in your title, people can find you immediately.

In a moment, I'll instruct you on how to completely customize your URL. You can even do this if you have a free account. As we're scrolling down looking at this person's LinkedIn account, I'm checking to see if they have a description of their company. I want to confirm if this person took the time to enter the descriptions needed, so it reads well. For the most part, when we're gauging someone's account I know if they took the time to put in a couple of paragraphs, they care about their business. If they slapped together a sentence, I don't want to see that. In addition, take a minute to peruse their featured skills and endorsements. I recommend that you scope out at least five of their listed skills.

If they haven't been endorsed for their skills yet, I'm fine with that, as long as they've posted five skills. You can keep moving forward once you've ascertained that is the truth. Keep scrolling on their profile until you get to their interests. Then click on "See All" to view the types of groups they're involved in. It's integral to know this because we are going to use this information to break the ice when we first make contact.

"Group" is the middle tab, but if you don't see that tab, then you will know they haven't taken time to join any groups. LinkedIn allows you to join up to 100 groups for free with a basic account, so go ahead and join as many groups as possible. If you and I are not connected yet on LinkedIn, I have two profiles, connect with me on both of them, and then you can see all the real estate related groups I'm in. You should join all these groups, too, because that's where you'll find a lot of your future and potential connections.

Once your prospective contact has met your guidelines, you can send them a message. But, before you dash off a note you'll want to take a minute to make sure you can send it in such a way that it's different than clicking "Connect." We're going to add a personalized message. Whenever you send an invitation, you have the option to customize it and make it more personal. We're not going to click "Send now." We're using the second option: "Add Note."

The message I will teach you allows 70 percent of your invited connections to accept your connection. Here's the message: "Hi Randall, I recently came across your profile and noticed we're members of several real estate-related groups. I'm looking to connect with like-minded professionals, such as yourself, and look forward to connecting and talking soon. Thanks, Jason."

If you don't add a personal message, you're extending yourself using the default setting for LinkedIn, which says,

"I'd like to add you to my professional network." My non-customized invitations have not gotten strong results with high-level individuals. If time goes by and you're not seeing people connect with you within 24 to 48 hours, they probably don't have a very strong presence or active account.

If you want to manage your network, click on "My Network." At the top of your network page click "Manage All." You'll see and be able to manage your invitations here. You can view the invitations you've received, and the ones you've sent. Click on the ones you have sent. If you've sent numerous invites, but you haven't heard anything back, you can click on the button that says, "Withdraw" the invitations you've sent. If people want to connect with you, they'll send you an invitation to connect.

After 48 hours, I recommend you click the withdraw button and begin again looking for the right types of folks you want to connect with.

Now, I'll tell you how to customize your URL profile. On your homepage, click on your profile. Next, click on the little pencil that allows you to edit your information. Under your contact and personal info, you'll see the option to update your URL for your individual account.

In addition to locating the professionals you need for your team, LinkedIn is a rich resource for cash buyers. If I want to connect with other real estate investors, I'll click on "People" then select my second and third connections. Everything we've already talked about earlier in this chapter applies. Note the profile picture, that the URL has been properly set up, etc. If this contact has listed skills but skipped the background photo and the URL, I'd still like to connect with them. This is why it certainly helps your reputation and perception to be a part of groups.

The message we're sending to real estate investors isn't going to vary much from the message that we sent to the asset manager. I'll click "Connect," then the "Add Note" button. Then I would add the same message as before. We'll change it up slightly, for our cash buyer, the person that I would like to invest in transactions with me. The message is: "Hello, Natalie and Dave, I came across your profile and noticed we're members in a lot of the same real estate-related groups. I'm coming across deeply discounted properties in your area and wanted to see if you'd be interested in doing business together. Talk soon, Jason."

Again, the messages we use and recommend are very short, and very to the point, and we fire them off as quickly as possible. The main reason we keep our notes short is that people don't want to take a look at an extremely long text. It takes them out of their frame of mind of what they're doing. Stating my intention clearly and concisely is what people want to read. Once they get your message, they'll check out your profile as well. That's where our advice comes full circle. You must also take the time to optimize your LinkedIn account. Load up your profile picture; list at least five skills, and then join at least five real estate-related groups.

Once you're connected, you'll get their phone number, email address, birthdate, website information and any other phone numbers associated with their account. That's important because you could pick up the phone and start calling people, or if you have their email, you can send them an email.

When it's their birthday, you could send out a personalized message, saying, "Hey Dave, I saw that it's your birthday, wanted to wish you a happy birthday. Hope all is well, reach out when you'd like to do some business together." Once more, don't make your note complicated. When you gain access to information on LinkedIn, you bypass going down to the county recorder's office, or getting the information for the real estate investor; you can avoid sending out a direct mail piece. I have nothing against doing any of those things, we have people in our office who do that, but eight times out of 10, because the individual is on LinkedIn, we omit that step as we rapidly assemble our cash buyers' list.

All you need is 8-12 people who want to buy properties in your area. Once that's sealed, you can call or email them when you have a deal. Maybe their website lists deals for you. And you don't need to post every single day. But it is a smart idea. I recommend if folks don't have ton of properties, they can still keep their face in front of people by using a site like brainyquote.com. Grab some quotes and put one up each day. Doing it takes less than two minutes, and people will keep seeing you, and they will get to know who you are, as well as that you're providing a constant reminder to them to do business with you.

If you are reaching out to a hedge funds manager, you can follow my same system. Type in "hedge fund" on LinkedIn and watch the people and companies it pulls up. If I click on a company, it'll allow me to see all the different employees working for that company. I can then reach those people. It's cool because I can connect with any person there.

If you're looking for people in a designated company, type in the company name, click on the company, and then view all the employees. Conducting searches in this way allows you to save yourself a ton of time. We want to save time whenever we can because isn't this one of the reasons you're educating yourself on real estate investing? If you think about it, it's our "why." Time gives us moments with our family and friends; it permits us to take that vacation we've always wanted. Maybe we can fill more of our schedules with charity work like we do. Being able to give back and operating a purpose-driven company is a possibility when you work the deals I've discussed in this book. You can do so much more with your business, but with yourself as well, which will give you the balance you need, a balance a lot of other real estate investors don't have. So, go out there. Make it happen with LinkedIn. If you want to rip off and duplicate anything I've told you, you have my permission to do that.

Whatever will shortcut your success, apply it to your strategy and get to your goals faster.

Chapter 12: Two Flipping Resources (One's a Secret!)

"Develop success from failures. Discouragement and failure are two of the surest stepping stones to success." - Dale Carnegie

At the time of this publication, the number one search engine is Google. Google can be used for far greater purposes than just searching for different shops or items you can purchase. It is the directory of everything you want to view at your fingertips. In your business, you can find deals and buyers with the simple insertion of a few keywords which we'll review in this chapter. You're about to learn how to go onto real estate investors' websites to find the types of deals and cash buyers required to run your business.

On Google, click in the field where you can type in any word or multiple words. You don't need a mile-long list of keywords for your industries because you'll pull the same data for the sites you need with our top keywords.

The number one keyword is "sell my house." Two is "buy my house." Three is "we buy houses." Four is "need to sell my house." These are the highest-performing top four. Now, the secret for finding folks in your specific area is to use the keywords and then add your city to the end. For example, I would use "sell my house Indianapolis," and that would pull up the searches I need access to, so I can find the websites most useful me. If I put in "sell my house Indianapolis" and I check out the search results, there are over 9.8 million previews for "sell my house Indianapolis."

And every ad listed will not be based in Indianapolis. I might encounter nationwide companies who are trying to rank their cities nationally. That's why it's important to look at more than the first three to four because those results will usually be Google ads anyway. These are people who have bought placements for "sell my house Indianapolis." As you scroll down the page, you'll come to a map, and it will display individuals who are local to your area. For this example, we're using Indianapolis, and Google has returned many different sources.

I want to click on "we buy Indy houses." Once I do, I've got a phone number I can use, and residence address. If they have a business address, they'll give that to me, too as well as any reviews for the website. Click, and you'll see other web results similar within Indianapolis.

If you want to learn if they have any deals, or you're looking for them to be cash buyers, when you call them you would say the following, "Hello, my name's Jason Lucchesi. I was on Google, and I was typing in 'sell my house Indianapolis.' I came across your listing, and I wanted to give you a call because I'm looking for real estate transactions I can purchase for my company. Would you be at all interested in looking or do you have any properties potentially for me?"

If you wanted to talk to determine the possibility of working with cash buyers your script would sound like, "Hello, my name's Jason Lucchesi. I saw your ad listed on Google, and I wanted to give you a call because I saw some of the reviews folks have left for you. I also took a look at your website, and I wanted to reach out to you, and let you know that I'm a real estate investor as well. I come across properties that would be perfect for a joint venture with you. Would you be at all interested in looking at some of the deals I have to see if we can do any type of a partnering?"

Spin your spiel in a way that works for you. As long as you hit the high notes, you will be successful. These calls could go one of two ways. You could either find somebody with properties for you or if they are a cash buyer, they might be combined as a seller and a buyer for you. When it comes to finding individuals on Google, you want to use that simplified approach again.

Think of these scenarios as if you were driving alongside the road and saw a bandit sign. A bandit sign is a cut out on a wooden pole. The methodology is the same whether you find info for a buyer on a physical sign or on Google (an online sign.) If you see bandit signs on the side of the road for the "we buy houses" people or the "ugly house" people, call them. Use the scripting in this chapter to talk to them; you can find out exactly what their wants and needs are. When you do this, you have a superior set of tools to start utilizing immediately.

It's all free, too. You can go to Google or any search engine such as msn.com or yahoo.com at any time. You might even be able to go to aol.com if it still exists. Any search engine will process this information. Wherever you go, you will likely see the exact same data as Google. Cruise those search engines for your results and then reach out!

Different keywords will give you different results. If I type in "we buy Indianapolis houses," Google returns completely different findings than when I entered "sell my house Indianapolis."

User-friendly sites give you the option of entering your first name, last name, email, phone, full property address, and when you do this, you could actually get an offer on your property. The site I'm on right now has a video and some testimonials. I want to find out if they have any current inventory. You can ask if they have any available inventories, to decide if they are a good source where you can purchase properties.

Let me give you another bonus. I know of a sort-of secret site to help you find both buyers and sellers. Not a lot of people are aware of gosection8.com. This site has a little search engine box just like Google. But it's only for people with properties who are seeking Section 8 tenants.

If you're not familiar with what Section 8 is, it's basically a program provided through the government that gives housing assistance to individuals unable to provide a living for themselves. The government allows them to use a Section 8 voucher, and landlords with properties they're looking to rent out can list their properties. Type in the city where you're looking to do business. Entering "Indianapolis, Indiana" shows me all 196 affordable rentals within my area.

Properties on gosection8.com are listed by either property managers or the actual owner of record. They're looking for people to provide their voucher. Sometimes, the listings say, "No voucher necessary," meaning the listed property is open to both Section 8 tenants and regular tenants without vouchers. The property I'm looking at right now is a three-bedroom, two bath house. They're asking for $1,150 per month in Indianapolis, in the Marion County area, which is central Indiana.

When you scroll down on the profile, you'll see all the property details. You'll even see a property description. I'm reading that this place has been freshly remodeled. And I've got a phone number, and email address. I'm also noting a phone number for RHSS Rentals, an 855 number. If you scroll down on the property description, there's a phone number for someone else named Victoria as well.

Call them up, and state the following, "Hello, my name's Jason Lucchesi. I came across your listing on gosection8.com. The property that is at 3611 Cork Bend

Drive. I'm giving you a call because I have properties that are very similar. I know this one is a three-bedroom, two-bath, and I wanted to see if you guys might be interested in looking at other properties like this one. They're almost within the same area, not too far from each other. Are you interested in substantial discounts?"

If you reach a rental company, they might say, "I don't make those types of decisions." Then I would say, "Can I speak to the individual who does because I'm going to recommend that they use you for their property management company, so this would be a win-win for everybody involved, especially if you're placing people in these properties. This would be a great Section 8 property." That's a shrewd way to get past the person on the phone if they're just the property manager.

When you're talking to property managers it can go a couple of different ways. You can get the information for the owner of record when they reply, "Let me talk to the owner, see if they're interested in looking at purchasing any additional properties." It's fine to proceed this way, but make sure you have some sort of a system in place, so you can properly follow up with them. If you're using Google, set a reminder for yourself on the calendar. Then you can contact them if they don't call you back. *Always* get a time when you can contact them again.

If I'm talking to John on the phone, and he states, "I'm going to have to contact the owner, see if they're interested." Your best reply is, "How long do you think that's going to take? Do you think I could contact you tomorrow, or would the next day be better?" If they say, "The next day would be better." You say, "Okay, great. I've got 10:00, 10:30 and 11:00 available on my schedule. Which time works best for you?" Then they'll let you know.

You could also say, "What works best for you as far as me following up with you? Morning, afternoon or evening?" When they tell you make sure you have your schedule in front of you so if they say, "Afternoon," you can rattle off three times that work. Always give three times because response studies have shown that people love to have three options. They usually go with the middle choice. After being in sales for 15 plus years, doing mortgages and real estate as well as reading numerous studies over the course of my career, I know whenever you give somebody three different options it's highly probable they will choose the middle one.

If you're going to talk to a property manager, you could say, "I'm giving you a call about your property on 3611 Cork Bend Drive. I'm a real estate investor. I saw that you're the property manager that has this property listed on gosection8.com. I wanted to find out from you if you have other properties like this for sale because we're looking for properties that are very, very similar Do you have properties like this for sale, or is the individual you're doing the property management for looking to potentially sell any of their properties they currently have?"

Now, the property manager knows you're an investor. You're looking for properties. If the owners do have properties, who's going to be the first one who gets notified? The property manager. If I'm an investor, the property manager is managing my properties, and I'm letting the property manager know because, typically, in contracts, they have the first right to list the property for sale or for rent. They're going to know if properties are for sale, so why not talk to them before the properties go on the market? You could get the property completely off-market, and if you're buying a property from another investor without a tenant, it means the property can't be labeled as income-producing, so you can snatch it up at a hefty discount.

The search I did in the Indianapolis, Indiana area pulled up 196 listings. It would obviously take you a long time to call all those people. I would recommend you use a software like Slybroadcast to handle this volume. You can enter the phone numbers for each contact on Slybroadcast, and instead of dialing 196 people you or your assistant can upload an Excel spreadsheet of all your phone numbers onto the site. The great news is that it's also very inexpensive.

Use Slybroadcast to record a message that will go right into a voicemail box. If someone is busy, and they hit the hang up button, it can be hard for them to see they missed a call. Instead of being intrusive, your message will go right to voicemail. When they are ready to listen to your voicemail, they'll hear what you have to say.

If we're calling people on gosection8.com, we would say something along these lines: "Hey there, it's Jason Lucchesi. I wanted to give you a call. I saw that you had a property listed on gosection8.com. I'm very interested in speaking to you about it. Please give me a call back. My phone number is 317-blah, blah, blah, blah, blah, blah." It can be short and sweet as I always advise you to do. You don't have to talk about a specific property.

When you call multiple investors make sure you have a point of reference. If I'm going to call both GoSection8 people and Google contacts, who might be my new JV partners, I want to make sure these lists are separated. You can make one list for GoSection8 people containing the phone number of the address associated with the property.

Then I would make a separate list for Google people, where I would record their phone number and website address. When you have this information on hand, you can easily say, "I was giving you a call in reference to your website. I'm a real estate investor here in town, and I'm reaching out to other investors because we're looking to buy, and I wanted to see if you had any properties that were available."

Such a simple plan will put you in a winning position. Make sure you have the phone number associated with their website, and at this stage of the game, I would highly advise you to start looking for your JV partners using the process I explained in recent paragraphs.

Gosection8.com people could be property managers, or they could be owners of record of the actual property. They could be buying or selling. If you've got a buyer primed to purchase properties that already have income from Section 8 vouchers, it's a great opportunity for you. You could contact these people and discover they have a package of 10 income-producing properties You could transact a package deal and make $20,000, $30,000, or even $40,000 off a single deal.

We've done it, and you can do it, too. We love seeing people use gosection8.com because so many people aren't utilizing this site, and everything's there for you: the phone number, the email address, and any other contact information. Using the site doesn't cost a penny. As you are choosing your handful of strategies to implement in your new business, I want to impress upon you to use this site to make real money and potentially close multiple deals.

Chapter 13: Working with Flipping Title Companies

"Success depends in a very large measure upon individual initiative and exertion and cannot be achieved except by a dint of hard work." - Anna Pavlova

Building your team and having the right resources at your fingertips is mandatory if you want to move forward in your real estate investing business. I would encourage you to have an investor-friendly title company, or attorney if you're in an attorney-close state, on your team. These people are invaluable to you when it comes to doing your investor transactions.

Big title companies aren't as flexible as mom and pop type investor-friendly title companies or attorneys because they don't want to do things in a non-traditional manner. They want traditional closings. They want multiple transactions to close consistently and constantly. That's not to say the mom and pop type companies aren't doing a lot of business, too, because a lot of them are.

We've established quite a few closing attorneys and companies in Indianapolis, but whenever we mentor a student or enter into a different market to do business, we've learned the best way to find these contacts is through referrals. Alternately, you can use sites like LinkedIn, Facebook, YouTube, and Google, which we'll review within this chapter.

You can set yourself up to receive referrals from attorneys, real estate agents, insurance agents, and other investors. You could go to your local real estate investors associations and meet an investor-friendly title company. When you do, you will talk to them, and see if they can do the types of transactions you specialize in. If you're primarily going to be doing wholesaling and if you're going to be using an assignment contract, you want to talk to them about assignments. You want to talk to them about doing A to B, B to C transactions, and sometimes you may need to use what's called an escrow agreement, which allows your end buyer to fund your first transaction. It's completely legal. Just talk to your title company, to make sure that they're using an appropriate insurance underwriter to ensure your title is fully insured. More than likely, you will find out this information from your closing representative who has a close relationship with their underwriter.

As an aside, I don't like using assignment contracts because if you're not a licensed real estate sales person, down the road, your cut will be deemed commission. If you're collecting commission without an actual license, you could get into trouble. So, to cross all your "t's" and dot all your "i's," talk to your attorney, so if you want to do assignment contracts, you will be legally clear to do so.

Title companies also know who's buying and selling properties within your area. When I started closing transactions back in the middle of 2008, we were with a strong investor-friendly title company; they started recommending different types of private money lenders we could use. After six months or so, we talked to them to reveal the people they worked with who were doing any type of lending. We were given referrals for individuals doing both hard money and private money loans. It turned out to be a really great opportunity for rehabs, too. Remember, there are always additional profits to be earned on rehabs.

I'm not saying don't do rehabs, but if you're just getting started as a real estate investor, I always encourage that you close eight, nine, and even 10 wholesale transactions before you start doing rehabbing. You need to learn the inside and outside parts of what it takes to get a transaction closed from A to Z. There are moving parts with rehab deals, so unless you have experience as a contractor or you're very handy and can get the house into a selling condition within a short period of time, I would encourage to do a few wholesale transactions first. You can gain this experience in a month or two. Closing eight to 10 transactions doesn't take long to do, especially when you use the strategies in this chapter. And if you want to sharpen your skills even more, you can always attend GetMyFlippingTraining.com. Check out some of our free training, and spend some time absorbing the right exit strategies. Performing the right exit strategies means you can make the most money from each of your transactions.

Pulling private money and hard money from a title company is an excellent plan. If they're an investor-friendly title company, they're likely doing a lot of the investors' deals in the local area, and that means you can find out the details. The title company won't hand over such information to you, so you can get around this by saying, "I'm going to give you my contact information. Can you pass along my information to the buyers you know?" Some people might feel a little weird about confidentiality, and I completely get it. You should get it, too. Understand some people don't give their information out to anyone. You can feel free to give them a card or shoot them an email. They'll forward your email over to their contact if they're interested. Then the buyers can reach out to you.

Title companies receive information from real estate agents; they receive information from other attorneys and are privy to upcoming properties. Title companies also have access to public records, and that equals more properties for you. They can search recently filed divorces, bankruptcies and AODs (affidavit of deaths) as well as probates. They also work with insurance agents, who, as we've discussed in a previous chapter, can prove to be an invaluable source for damaged properties in a very distressed state. Opportunities exist for you because owners of record want to unload these properties in a hurry.

Title companies can alert you whenever a quit claim has been filed, meaning information has been altered on the title. If a husband and wife were on the title, it means they were joint tenants. But if one of them passed away, then only one would remain on the title. We'll discuss the AOD (that would need to be filed in this instance) in greater detail when we go over the probate chapter shortly.

In the case of a death, you can reach the appropriate contact right away. That person will usually be called a beneficiary. The individual filing the quit claim has had a loved one pass away. The best action you can take is to reach out to them and see if they're interested in potentially selling. You must be sensitive and not call like a callous shark to purchase their house the day after their spouse passed away.

I recommend approaching these people with a direct mailer. Your mailer can be vague. You won't say anything about the death. You would talk about being interested in purchasing the property. The less information you state that you know, the better. The people who have lost their loved one might be a little bit older and might have children. They could have grandchildren. They probably don't need their house anymore. It might be too big. The remaining spouse might want to downsize, or move to an assisted living facility, and so they may be open to selling the property.

We've seen it dozens of times, where the individual has no idea what to do after a death. They go to assisted living and six months down the road want to sell the property. Then an agent comes in and doesn't know exactly what to do either because mom or dad left the property and didn't move all their stuff. They didn't properly winterize the property, and now it's a big mess. There are potential roofing issues now. There might be flooding from the property being vacant for six months. When this happens, it's because the person trying to hold it all together is somewhat in a shocked state of mind from losing their love or partnership of decades. I can't stress enough that you need to be delicate. Use your mailers and give the title company the task of finding you the information you need by searching public record.

Once you get hooked up with the right buyers, you could find out if they have any potential properties they're looking to liquidate. A lot of individuals do liquidate their properties after they've had them for a bit. One situation might be that someone's doing a rehab and then they want to sell it at retail. We don't want to do a transaction with them because we don't want to buy the rehab. We're looking to buy properties at discounts, not at retail.

You could connect with a buyer with a portfolio of 40 properties. We recently talked to somebody with 40 properties, and they wanted to sell off five properties at a time mainly because they were ready to retire. When someone wants to exit real estate, you can land some fantastic deals. They're older, they've made a ton of money, and they just want to relax. They don't want to worry about tenants. They don't want to worry about property managers. They want to relax, retire, and take up the pastimes they've been dreaming about for years. Some folks don't know how to properly manage their properties. It could leave them with a lot of headache and heartache.

Look to the title company to connect you with not only buyers, but sellers. As I've stated in a previous chapter, when you're in the search field on LinkedIn and you're attempting to find an investor-friendly title company, type in title company, and then locate people specifically in your area.

On Facebook, you'll want to find people in real estate groups. You could state, "Hi, my name's Jason. I'm here in Indianapolis. I'm looking for an investor-friendly title company. Does anyone have any recommendations?" Go specifically to groups in your area and type in your question. If I'm in Indianapolis, I want to find geo-targeted groups on Facebook specifically for real estate investors in my hometown. You can find and get referrals using this tactic as well.

YouTube is like LinkedIn, but you'll type in the title company and then your city. I'll type in "title company Indianapolis." Or, "investor-friendly title company." You might also want to search "real estate closing coordinator." It will give you the people with videos. You'll receive results where people might've talked about closed transactions, testimonials, and results for attorneys and real estate agents.

YouTube can prove to be a great avenue for finding the right type of investor-friendly title company. Just make sure that they can close your wholesale transactions. You want to specifically know they can close A to B, B to C transactions. Even if they can't do the escrow agreement, you can line up funding for an A to B, B to C transaction through besttransactionfunding.com to get funding for a day. I believe you'll have to pay 1.75 percent on money you borrow. It's very cheap money. We know the owner extremely well. He will get your transactions done quickly. Make sure in the referral box you let them know we sent you, because you'll get a discount on the fees, and you'll also get your transaction closed much faster.

You'll have unlimited proof of funds letters from them as well. The owner, Dwayne, has set it up so you will start making money quickly. You don't have to worry about getting a long loan. They don't have to pull your credit. They just want to make sure you have your end buyer in place. If your title company is unable to do an escrow agreement, move to an A to B, B to C transaction, or again, use the assignment contract.

When I first started as a real estate investor and found a relevant title company, I didn't have much money for an attorney to review my documents. So, I went to the investor-friendly title company, and they reviewed all my documents. They put the fees for that attorney onto my first transaction. It actually saved me quite a bit of money upfront, and it was money I didn't have since I was living on weekly unemployment checks, and I ran through that money because of my bills.

If you don't have the funds readily available for attorney costs, you can see if the investor-friendly title company would be willing and able to do what I did. Most of them are eager to help you. If they're not, then go to another investor-friendly title company. You should know your title company's capability already and have asked them what they can do for you when you begin working together. You want them on your team and will need to know how they will work to close transactions. What better way to make sure all your needs are met than to secure the right title company. Find a title company that can handle your business as well as give you referrals for cash buyers, deals, private money, hard money, and your pipeline could literally grow every day.

Chapter 14: The Flipping Absentee Homeowners

"Failure is a great teacher, and I think when you make mistakes and you recover from them and you treat them as valuable learning experiences, then you've got something to share." - Steve Harvey

Individuals with a good amount of capital within their bank account, not making them as much money as they want, often become investors in real estate. They may not want to do the wholesaling, rehabbing or any other deals. But they might want to buy properties that will create cash flow for them and bring them a solid return on investment they're not seeing from other sources such as the stock market, money market, Bitcoin, and other accounts, or investments.

They'll invest into properties and see the funds come in from rentals. I'll give you a real quick case study. We work with people all the time who purchase properties in Indianapolis from Hawaii, Canada, Europe and all over the world. They purchase properties here because we have such a high-performing cash flow ratio. You can buy 10 properties for the cost of maybe 1 very, very, very, very tiny property in

California. But you can get 10 or 12 properties for $300,000 in Indiana that will cash flow well for you.

They might have $100,000 and want to find property to invest in, but where they go wrong is they neglect to attend a coaching program, or they haven't gone through training on purchasing properties and hiring property managers. They'll do all the rental stuff. They'll do all the screening, or hopefully, some sort of screening. They'll get a tenant. But the next thing you know, they're in Hawaii with a property or two in Indiana. When they're not on the scene, the tenants leave. The owners can't find anybody else, and they don't know how to handle their problem.

In this particular case, whether a tenant lives on the property or not, the property is called an absentee homeowner property. This is where the owner of the property is absent from the actual subject property. It's not considered a property they live in as a primary residence. It won't even be considered a vacation or a rental.

As an absentee homeowner, the property is subject to a lot of different happenings. If the property goes unmaintained, we're going to see tall grass, vandalism and exterior theft; we might notice missing air conditioning units. This happens quite a bit if your property is in what's called C and D class neighborhoods. C and D class neighborhoods are comprised of low-income class earners to lower-middle-income class earners. Most residents have been there for a long time. But like most neighborhoods, some people just don't intend to do the right thing. This is the advent of the disrepair state, with vandals and thieves setting upon the property and inflicting damage.

You can get ahold of these absentee homeowners and buy these properties at substantial discounts. Find their information through code violations. If the grass exceeds a certain length, the county will put violations on their property until mowed down to a normal standard.

If the property has broken windows, they'll slap on a code violation. If vandalism has not been remedied: code violation. A missing air conditioner is also a code violation.

Violations differ from county to county and state to state. You could learn about code violations at your county recorder. Review the recent code violations within your county that are public record. Once you find out who the code violation is filed against, access the mailing address. You don't want the actual property address; you want to find the mailing address for the individual who received a code violation.

As covered in prior chapters, when you want to track someone down you can use Spokeo, or TLO to skip trace. When you get their information, you can call them or send out a direct mail piece. Again, I like to be as short and sweet as possible on my yellow letters. Being able to send out a handwritten yellow letter to your potential prospect has always been a great strategy for getting people to call you back. We typically use a regular 8.5 x 11 piece of yellow legal pad paper, and we use red fine-tip marker for the text we write on the paper. The response rate we typically receive using the method is around 21-23 percent. You can follow this format: "Hi, (their name), I'm interested in purchasing your property at 123 Main Street. We can close fast and with cash. If you're interested, give me a call at blah-blah-blah. Thanks, (your name)." Below your name, write your phone number. When you do it on a yellow letter, people pay attention, in a positive way.

If a person tends to move quite a bit, TLO and Spokeo will be on their information pretty quickly as compared to the county issuing the code violation.

You can learn about these properties through property managers also. Sometimes if the property manager's communication with the owner of record is spotty, they might have a strategy that will benefit you. Therefore, you need to contact the property manager and say, "I noticed the owner lives in Washington and it doesn't look like the property's been well-maintained. I'm not sure if there's an issue with tenants coming into it." Then the property manager can go mow and take measures, so the property will not be vandalized, and there will be no code violations.

What if a tenant moves out after destroying the interior of the home? It's up to the owner of record to repair the inside of the property. If massive damage occurs, the property manager can't place somebody in the property. If the property manager doesn't have a tenant, they're not going to get paid. If they're not getting paid, there's no incentive for them to mow the lawn and resolve any vandalism.

It would be in the best interest of the property manager for us to work together to get the property sold. If there is work needed, the owner may not want to do it. If there are code violations adding up and you've talked to the property manager, and they tell you, "This person has no interest in keeping this property anymore. We're having a tough time trying to fill it," you can direct the conversation toward selling. Maybe the property manager is trying to sell, and he's not getting any bites. Sometimes, the property doesn't go on the market, because the owner doesn't want the property manager to sell it. If we can do a private sale through an off-market channel, and through the property manager, it's a clever way to pick up the property. It would be an easy wholesale or rehab, especially at the right discounted price.

Other individuals that you can turn to for leads are real estate agents. They'll know if some of their clients have purchased properties and it's not going as planned, especially if they're struggling with the property management themselves. If you're not a property manager, you shouldn't become a property manager. Hand off those tasks to the professionals and let them take care of the property for you. Trust me. I've been there. I've done that. It's much more favorable to appoint someone else to handle those messy details.

The attorneys you work with will also know about clients. Maybe there was a divorce, and a property was abandoned. Maybe the property couldn't get sold, and neither party truly cares about it. If you raise your hand and say, "I'm going to take care of this for you. The code violations are going to be paid and resolved," your attorney will let their client know that they don't have to worry about the property anymore. They'll assure the owner you will attend to every aspect of the property, so the owner can move on. Being able to have their attorney point them in the right direction with getting a problem solved helps out tremendously with alleviating stress. And, having the attorney give a strong recommendation only gives the property owner even more peace of mind knowing everything will be taken care of.

Let's say you're on the road driving for dollars. If you find specific areas you want to do business in, you can go to those particular locations and do what's called "blanket driving." Simplified, this means you are driving around and going from street to street. If you see properties that aren't being maintained with faded paint, a ragged roof, or if you're in the Midwest, you might spot hail damage, those are sensible prospective properties for you. We know if there's hail damage, and nothing has been fixed, it's another sign the property is completely absent, and the person doesn't want anything to do with it anymore.

Don't drive around just to drive around. Make sure you're strategic and not wasting time or gas. Plot out the paths where you will go. Goggle Maps is an accurate tool that can assist you in planning your route to make sure you're going in and out of the right neighborhoods, and that you will see the types of properties high on your list.

If you're going to be wholesaling properties, you'll want to be in the areas where the C and D class properties are located. If you're unfamiliar with these cities and neighborhoods, use the MLS to identify where a good amount of properties in your C and D class neighborhoods are being sold. You want to find out which areas have high amounts of cash transactions. Pulling that information and finding out the actual owner address is imperative, so you can reach out to the owner and broach the selling conversation.

Use listsource.com, yellowletterscomplete.com, or pioneerinfo.net to find homeowners. These are paid services. When you're paying for information, you want to double check and ensure the information is accurate before you do any mailing.

Spokeo and/or TLO are excellent and reliable sources to cross reference the information you receive elsewhere.

I work from home and to approve my account with TLO they needed to know I've got doors to my office that lock with a key. If you have a file cabinet in your office, it also needs to have a lock and key. They will also want to make sure your computer is password protected. Because you are getting highly sensitive information, they will do a background check on you, to confirm nobody could enter your office and use that information.

Spokeo allows you to sign up and go. Establishing your account will not require as thorough a process as TLO. Spokeo may not provide the most accurate information but my wife loves it for our properties. She swears it's always accurate.

Before you commit, you can do trial runs on those programs. TLO does allow a two-week trial. Spokeo offers very inexpensive searches, so you might want to try it out. See which one works best for you and then sign up for whichever one you prefer. Absentee homeowners can be a surprisingly lucrative source, because a lot of people think, *oh, they live out of state*. Some folks get a bad taste in their mouth when they don't understand how to go about securing a rental property, and so they never progress in the deal any farther than thinking about it.

It takes getting a property manager in place and making sure that that property manager knows what they're doing. If you're going to do this the right way, plan on selling the properties as income-producers. Understand, you might need to mow the lawn and do minor stuff around the house. If you're going to search for a property manager, make sure that they're managing a minimum of 200 houses or more within your particular area. Get three to five referrals for individuals you can call so you'll receive your money on time, every single month. You shouldn't have any repair issues either. If tenants say, "That property manager is great," they're more than likely lying. Most people don't receive payments on time every single month, especially if you're calling five different people, so just be aware of that insider tip.

You want to confirm evictions are being done the right way. The property management company should pull proper information and conduct screening for new tenants. Regarding similar properties, they should know confidently what a vacancy loss will be. If you did a 12-month contract, and people left after a month or two, it may take the property manager 30 days to put a new tenant in the property. Your property manager should not just look out for their own interests.

Property managers are going to want first month's rent as their way of getting started. And then they're going to want 8-10 percent of monthly rent from that standpoint. You need them on your team because in many cases, they will have the inside scoop on properties for sale, and this allows you to purchase at a really steep discount.

We work with absentee homeowners frequently to seal deals, especially those who are out-of-state. They simply don't want the properties anymore and are ready to let them go at substantial discounts. Just the other day we were speaking to a new property manager we found through gosection8.com, and this individual knew of a couple dozen properties an owner wanted to sell as quickly as possible. Reaching out to property managers can help you develop a gigantic pipeline of deals you can flip for big profit checks.

Chapter 15: What About Flipping Probates?

"There are people who make things happen, there are people who watch things happen, and there are people who wonder what happened. To be successful, you need to be a person who makes things happen." - Jim Lovell

The Definition of Probate

Before we dive too deeply into the topic of probate, let's first define probate's meaning. Probate is the legal process that occurs when a person dies, and their assets are distributed. This encompasses all manner of their property, including real estate (residential, personal, and commercial). Property can span from furniture and cars to collectible basketballs. Any item that the person owned at the time of their death can be considered property.

It is a common misunderstanding, that when a person has a will, they will be able to avoid the probate process. This is simply not true. Not only does a will not prevent the probate process, it, in fact, initiates and facilitates the probate process, to help it run faster and smoother and to make sure everything is done according to the will of the deceased.

All estates must go through a real estate process unless a living will has been set up. A living will means a trustee has been appointed who has ownership of the deceased's property. This living trust must be established prior to death. Probate does, however, prove the will is valid by assessment, that it has been signed, it is not fraudulent, and that it is the most current will.

A person may have several wills over the period of their lifetime. If they have been married more than once, had children, if they have gotten divorced, these are just a handful of life events that may cause a person to write, or rewrite a will. Sometimes a person may even have 2-4 wills over their entire lifetime. When this is the case, then the court will determine the validity of the will, and that it is the most current one.

Probate then pays the debts and taxes that were left behind by the deceased. One of the biggest benefits of buying probate real estate properties is that you can get pennies on the dollar. Not many real estate investors are educated in how to acquire probate properties, in adding them to their business, in working with them and closing them. Probate is a specialized field and requires very specific knowledge to ensure deals are managed correctly.

One of the misconceptions about probate is that it is challenging to close these deals. More often than not, difficulties in closing reflect a lack of education on the investor's behalf. It's not unrealistic to understand that most people don't know what probates are unless, a) they've gone through the probate process themselves, or b) they're an educated investor and working in probates. People experienced in handling probates may work in a courthouse, for example. They may have been exposed, as a third-party, to how the deals are processed.

By and large, most people know what probate is, but they don't fully understand how the process works. It is this lack of understanding that has led to the misperception of people saying, "It's tough to work probates. I don't want to deal with them in my business. I'm not going to add them to my portfolio." Thinking this way means missing out on the huge, huge benefits of understanding and working with probates.

How Probate Works

To successfully work in probate, you must first understand how it works. When people are in the process, you must fully comprehend the steps that will be taken.

First, the probate case is filed, and a case number is assigned. That case number is significant because knowing it will give you all the information you need as an investor.

That leads us to misperception #2 that these case numbers are difficult to locate. People have said, "I don't know how to find the case numbers. It's too hard. I don't want to do it."

Once you acquire that case number, it is incredibly easy to get all the information you need from the probate to facilitate and implement the deals into your business. If the will is valid, it is then entered into the probate file. The court next appoints an executor according to the will. If there is no will, the court will appoint an administrator.

An administrator/executor perform the same job, but they just have different names. The difference is that one was appointed by the decedent and the other was elected by the court. That is not the only difference between having a will

184

and not having a will. But it is one of the variances you could encounter in probate. Not everyone is familiar with the term "administrator." Most states just call that role the executor, no matter how they were appointed.

Next, the estate representative, the executor or the administrator will do the following: 1) search for all assets and debts, 2) appraise the assets, and 3) confirm the debts claimed against the estate. Anyone who has a debt they feel is owed to them for personal or business reasons can claim the entire estate. By the time the probate file is closed, they will have been paid off and the debt satisfied.

The process of confirming the debts ensures no unsubstantiated debts can be claimed against the estate. Once the court has appointed the executor, most states by law must publish a notice in the local paper that the decedent has died. This is because creditors will then see the news of the death and they can claim the estate if they are owed money.

The executor will then make sure the claim is legitimate and will make plans to pay off the debt. Once all the debts have been confirmed, the estate representative will liquidate the assets as necessary to satisfy these obligations. If the decedent has stocks, bonds, collectibles, cars, or anything of value that will help to satisfy the debts, they are liquidated to pay them off. They will do so according to the will, or according to the plans the family has decided upon.

Finally, they will resolve claims of debts and inheritance concerns. Claims, debts and estate issues refer to any anything that hasn't been substantiated or hasn't been fully proven. If a creditor has claims against the estate, and they're not considered legitimate, the executor must then verify or dispute these claims, by proving they're not legitimate, or coming to a settlement agreement with the creditor.

Inheritance Matters

When it comes to family, inheritance issues must be settled. This is another huge headache and can cause a lot of problems when the executor must decide who gets what. Sometimes, the family may not agree with the executor's decisions. Sometimes, the family can't agree on anything. As you can imagine, this can cause unbelievable problems.

These types of situations can be advantageous to you because the estate representative may just want to get rid of the property. When you come to them with a resolution, it will make everybody happy. You make it easy for them to get back to their family and say, "I found a way to solve this. We can get everyone paid off. We'll all be happy, and we won't have to worry about these stresses anymore." When you start working with the executor and the family, you offer them a desirable and unique solution to help them get out of their situation.

When it is time to close the case, the estate representative will prepare a final report on the will at the county for the submission to the court of beneficiaries. They will distribute the final assets and then close the case when there are no other outstanding debts against the estate.

You must have a living trust set up for the probate process. A living trust or a revocable trust will avoid the probate process and usually leads to a faster distribution of assets.

When this is the case, you can deal on a property that's never been listed. This means it's 100 percent off the market, and in most cases, it's been paid off. If you are so lucky as to find a property like this, then you don't have to worry about complications such as liens or tax debts. Usually, descendants are also ready to let the property go for a meager offer because they don't want to worry about it.

Learning the Probate File

You can find several different types of commercial and residential properties in probate. Single-family residences, condos, townhouses, manufactured homes and mobile homes, some of these properties may have been the primary residence of the decedent, some might be vacation homes or investment properties. You'll also find commercial properties ranging from multifamily buildings, industrial properties, vacant lots, pretty much anything that's categorized as a real estate property can be found in a probate file.

More properties mean more opportunities for you because not only will you have access to buy the primary residence (in most cases), but you will have access to potentially, a vacation home, a secondary residence, or any investment properties. The family dealing with these multiple properties has to worry about maintaining/rehabbing them and paying taxes. In most cases, they just want to unload these properties quickly.

The first item you will note when you open the probate file is the petition for application of probate. This form will give you a lot of information. It contains details about the deceased and the assets they've left behind. These lists are usually made by the executor and the attorney.

Locate the proof of publication in the file. You will see there is an inventory appraisal of all the property.

You may see a couple of different types of appraisals. You will not likely see both within one file, but one or two appraisals will be done. Either a professional appraiser will do a drive-by appraisal, where they will appraise the property from their vehicle and use comps within the area to develop a valuation, or a more in-depth appraisal will be done. In this scenario, the appraiser is hired to go through the property, take measurements and do a much more thorough job. You will receive a highly detailed evaluation of what the property is worth.

These appraisals are generally good for one year. If the appraisal is older than a year, the court will automatically assume that it is invalid and will order another one to be done.

Beyond the appraisal(s), you will also find within the file, the will of the deceased, notice to creditors (including any owed debt), and the order for probate—this form allows the probate to proceed.

Within the probate, you will find one of three different types of wills. The first and most common type of will is the witnessed will. This is what most people perceive when they hear the word "will." It's a typewritten, legal document that has been dated and signed by both the deceased and witnesses. Sometimes, you will notice within this document that no property will be mentioned.

The next type of will is what's called a holographic will. Many people are unfamiliar with this type of will, which is a handwritten, legal document, that has been dated and signed by the deceased. This will is not accepted in all states because it's handwritten, it hasn't been executed in an official setting, and it has simply been dated and signed by the deceased. Because anyone can write one up, they are often not accepted as an official, legal document.

The third kind of will that you may encounter is a nuncupative will. Yes, as they say, a verbal contract is binding. A nuncupative is basically an oral will that is used when a person has minimal assets they intend to leave behind. Encountering this will is rare, and it is also not accepted in all states.

Even though you may never see a holographic will or a nuncupative will, it is important that you are aware of them on the off chance you encounter one or both in probate deals.

The time to capitalize on the property is when the will is being read. This is a small window of opportunity and a limited time, so you want to make sure you read the will carefully and familiarize yourself with the language. Pay extra close attention to the testimony power of sale statement. If the wishes of the deceased are honored, no publication of any kind will be printed, except for the creditor notice. As a result, these properties have little exposure to the market, and you can capture them at steep discounts.

You will also want to gather all the information you will need on the heirs, like what percentage is going to whom, and who has been named the executor. When you learn the phone number, email, and physical address, you can start communicating with the person in authority and find out if there's any way you can help them. Also, within the will, you will find the notice to the creditors and a list of the deceased's descendants, who also may have an equitable interest in the estate.

How to Find Probate Leads

Knowing the tricks and tips of finding probate deals on the market will yield you the highest amount of profit possible. It's imperative that you focus on your strategy for finding the right types of probate leads that you can get under contract and flip very quickly. Every single probate deal will not be worth going after. It may or may not make sense, and you may not want to proceed after you learn the specifics.

The fact of the matter is that you will not be able to make a decent profit on every single probate deal. That's okay because you want to make sure your time is well spent. Concentrate on this for a moment: Time is one of the rarest and most precious commodities. It's something that you can't buy more of. This is why it's so important to choose your probate deal wisely.

I urge you to read further to learn about the two most popular types of wills that we see in the industry today. We'll go in-depth about the processes that are followed so you can rip them off and start using them in your business immediately.

Before we get to the nuts and bolts of these types of probates, let's briefly discuss the need to find a qualified attorney.

When dealing in probates, you need to work with an attorney who has estate planning expertise. Don't just snap up any old attorney specializing in the usual law categories like divorce or bankruptcy. It's fine if your attorney works in these areas in addition to possessing the qualifications to handle estate planning. But you need an expert who will understand your business. This will help you out substantially. When you meet with your attorney, let them know you're a real estate investor and that you can pull the trigger rapidly on the right types of investments. When you do that, it also complements your attorney and puts them in a positive light. Note: it's important to talk to more than one real estate planning attorney when you are getting started.

The reason why I stress finding an attorney who knows what they are doing and that you can trust is because they might be working not only with mom or dad on the estate, but the sons and daughters, too. They might even need to work with extended members of the family. This attorney will handle all the paperwork and the documentation; this attorney will handle all the court interaction. Get in with the right kind of attorney, and they will act as a great referral source for you if you are the go-to person who purchases properties from executors of estates.

The executor will deal with all the descendants and everyone else who is actually part of the estate. When you come in and begin talking about what you can do for everyone by purchasing the property, it takes a load off everybody's shoulders, including your attorney. When you help the attorney by making an offer and having that offer accepted by the executor of the estate, then you have just resolved a gigantic roadblock for them.

After dealing with a substantial amount of probates, I have noted about 75-80 percent of the time; most executors were caught off-guard. Maybe the death in the family was a surprise, and suddenly, they find themselves as the executor, in a bind and needing to take care of mom and dad's estate. They're trying to do the right thing in taking care of all the descendants. So, usually, they want to liquidate the estate as quickly as possible. The percentage of people who want to compile everything and sell it as soon as possible so they can move on is very high, about 90-95 percent.

I'm not saying you can come in and get the property for 10 cents on the dollar. You could, but the seller will want to get a fair price on the property, and when you break it down, there is not much difference between offering $150,000 and $200,000. You could get away with an offer of $150,000 for the simple fact that the sellers may want to liquidate the property and move on, so they might accept your first offer.

Remember, your attorney will be the one who is making the introductions (what we call a third-party endorsement) to the individuals whose family member has died and who are going through the probate process. The cycle is that someone passes away, an executor of the estate is appointed, and then your attorney will connect you with these parties. This might happen through a phone call or a meeting if the descendants want their attorney to be present, so they have a better idea of what to expect.

Once you do your first deal with your attorney, the attorney becomes familiar with how you work and what your process is, more importantly, when you complete a deal from start to finish, your attorney gains confidence. Then your attorney is going to open the floodgates for you. When you establish this relationship, it will likely lead to other opportunities not outlined in this chapter. Your attorney will also work with folks who are facing bankruptcy, divorce, foreclosure and other legal circumstances. You will probably receive referrals to these other people and situations once you have completed your first deal successfully and done what you said you were going to do.

If you want to find an attorney with a probate specialty, you can go to real estate investor associations. There is a plethora of other sources you can use as well. You can find lawyers on Facebook and LinkedIn. When you meet these people, you will be able to understand their mindset and expectations up front. This way there are no surprises. You will not be caught off-guard. LinkedIn is an excellent resource to find this type of attorney as well.

You can find attorneys on YouTube, too, by doing a similar search in the search engine box. When you type in "real estate attorney Indianapolis," (you can replace "Indianapolis" with your city), you'll be able to find lawyers in your area. You can get their phone number off the YouTube channel. They've got emails in their videos. And when you tell them how you found their information, it's a great icebreaker!

Don't forget about Google to find attorneys. Google is a great source and the biggest search engine in the world. Use the same search parameters you would to find an attorney on YouTube.

You can also work in probate virtually. For example, if you are in Boise, Idaho and you want to do business in Grand Rapids, Michigan, you absolutely can do that! All it really takes these days to work in this capacity is a laptop and phone.

In addition to getting referrals from your attorney, your title company can also send people and probates your way. You can find probates on public record, too. Go to the county clerk's office or find a county clerk's office online. A lot of counties are on the web now, and you can click on their sites to get the information you need.

When you go online or in-person to find your county office, you will need to know the names of the individuals, which can often be found by looking in the obituaries. You can look on newspaper sites. You can Google "recent deaths" and insert the name of the area where you are looking. For example, I would type "notice of deaths Indianapolis," or "notice of deaths Indianapolis industry."

Pull up the obituary that will give you details of the death. You can read the name of the person who died and their age. You can see their address and then do a more intensive Google search to find out even more information. Sometimes, you might even be able to learn the names of the survivors, and those survivors are the key contacts. Gather these living survivors and give them a call, send them an email, or pop a letter in the mail to ask about the property in probate.

Believe it or not, one of the best ways to get actual contact information is through a real skip tracing service. As mentioned in earlier chapters, simply enter the individual's name on the TLO website. You will be able to read their address and phone numbers when you start your search. You can also find extended family of the decedent if you need to:

sons, daughters, brothers, sisters, aunts, and uncles, no matter who is involved in the estate, you can find them. The sole reason you are performing this search is to reach out to these people and inquire about their property.

If you make a connection and are told, "I need you to talk to my brother," or "I need you to talk to my sister," that's great! Your contact will give you the information you need to get to the right person and start working the probate deal.

When you get the contact information, it will lead you to the case number. Once you have the case number, then you can get the mailing address, and find out who the executor is; you can also view the descendants.

Most of the time, you will see anywhere between 1-3 descendants in addition to the executor of the estate. When you develop a team, you can send people from your office to the county clerk's office to collect this information for you. I use about four county offices in working our probate deals, and you can certainly use more than one county clerk's office as well.

You may have heard that you can buy purchase list data. You must be careful if you choose to do this. Some states, including Indianapolis, are non-disclosure states. Meaning, some of the information that you would buy from a list provider isn't going to be 100 percent accurate. One of the places that I would recommend you try is listsource.com. This is an ideal site for you to reach out to the right people and follow up with a direct mail piece. Make sure you send out your direct mail piece before you start calling them.

I can tell you from experience that when you get your system down to predictable processes and when you have closed a few deals with your attorney, the leads will come in because your attorney will trust that you are a person of your word. The same concept applies when you start working with the county clerk's office, and you get comfortable knowing exactly what you are looking for to close the probate, from the first to the final step. The best thing about both resources is that they are free to use.

Skip tracing does cost money, and it is entirely up to you if you would like to invest in that resource. It's not necessary, but you will get results within a faster time frame.

The next strategy I will cover is what to do after you have a lead under contract, and I will discuss the smartest way to make the most amount of money and profit within the shortest period of time. These are called exit strategies, and we will learn all about them in the next section.

Getting the Probate Deal Closed

We've talked about the definition of probate, and how to find probate deals, now we can focus on getting the actual probate done. When you close a probate deal, you can go to the title company, or if you're in an attorney state, you can go through your attorney to receive your payment. Before we begin your exit strategy, however, it's imperative that we talk about the title. Always order the title work at your earliest convenience for any deal under contract. This is one of the very first things you need to do to make sure the title is clear. By clear, I mean that there aren't any judgments; there are no additional liens (because some of the liens may transfer from owner to owner). These individual liens are called municipality liens and federal tax liens, and you do need to take them into account. You absolutely must be aware of these items so order the title up front and immediately.

If you're unsure how to read a title report, have your title representative or attorney go over it with you. Their explanations will make it so much easier to understand, and you will learn the right way to read the title.

In addition to learning how to read the title and ordering it as soon as your deal is under contract, you will need to understand how a probate deal works from start to finish. The stages include getting the deal under contract, going to the closing table and collecting your check.

I recommend you use your own state-approved purchase and sales agreements. It's very simple to do. Every detail is laid out for you, and the documents have already been approved by your own state's attorneys. So, why not use forms that are already legal, transparent and ready to go? You can get these documents from title companies, your attorney, and real estate agents. They can give you blank purchase and sales agreements, and you don't have to pay for them.

You will want to keep in mind as I specify further about your exit strategy, that I personally do an A to B, B to C transaction, and that is what the next sections will reference.

Let me explain.

A is the current owner of record, the individual from whom you are purchasing the property. In this case, since it's probate, we are talking about the executor of the estate. The executor has the authority to sign on behalf of the deceased, because they have what's called power of attorney, meaning, they can sign to liquidate any property owned by the estate.

B is you as the investor in both scenarios, the first and second and transactions in the A to B, and in the B to C exchange.

C is going to be your end buyer. You will have two separate purchases and two separate sales agreements, that will allow you to flip the property the same day. It's all about full disclosure and full transparency.

If you follow the plan I lay out for you and use our friends over at besttransactionfunding.com, they will fund your transaction, and you will be successful in probates. The reason I like to do an A to B, B to C transaction is that it's clean and there is a clear and proper legal trail.

Before you get started, ensure that an attorney licensed in your state will review your actual transactions and documentation. There is a distinct reason that you need attorneys and it is simply because we are not attorneys; we are real estate investors. We need their expertise, so our probate deal will be legally executed.

Best Transactional Funding requires 3-5 business days to close. Sometimes, they may be able to expedite your closing, depending on your circumstances. I like to take advantage of this offering because I'm not a real estate agent and some states are getting tricky when it comes to using assignment contracts. Just make sure the document you're using will be reviewed by an attorney. In my opinion, the best way to schedule your transactions is to book your first closing, your A to B transaction, in the morning. You second transaction would ideally, take place in the afternoon.

You must make sure the transactional funder will either have their funds available that morning, or the day before your closing. This is a necessity you can't overlook. As a rule, have everything in place before you head to the closing table. Before you go, review the closing statement, make sure the taxes are accurate and make sure any fees such as closing costs and recording fees are correct. Don't forget that you should get a discount on your second transaction. Because both of your transactions will be done on the same day, you shouldn't have to pay for title insurance again. In fact, you should receive a substantially reduced fee since the title company or the attorney will not have to do a lot of different paperwork on the second transaction.

Making sure everything lines up accordingly on the settlement statement is going to be a key factor as well, so make sure you confirm this to be true. Your transactional funder, if you decide to use one, is going to charge anywhere between 1.5-1.875 percent of the actual purchase price—your purchase price from the owner of record. They may charge a processing fee, too, that could range anywhere from $400 to $500. The good news is, if anyone needs to see the proper chain of title, they can view it by public record. It will show that you were an actual owner, that you took ownership of the property and that you weren't just a middle man.

Now, if you are a real estate agent and you would like to use the assignment contract to receive a commission, you just need to follow whatever procedures are necessary for your brokerage—because most of the time, the commission's not going to be made out to you personally. It's going to be made out to your brokerage.

You may have received a referral from an attorney, and if that is the case, make sure you fully disclose that relationship and that everything is on the up-and-up.

But let's say you're unsure of where to get your deposit money, or you're unsure of where to get your earnest money deposit that your seller wants, so you can get your deal done.

That's the beauty of this type of transaction. We will receive our deposit money from our end buyer.

We'll use the following example to illustrate this analogy.

We have a deal for $100,000. The seller wants us to put $1,000 down in earnest money. At that point, we would put into the contract that we will give the owner of record the earnest money deposit and that it shall be deposited within 3-5 business days prior to the closing date. That's the language I typically use, but we can change our language and make the time shorter. I do this because I can have my cash buyer put funds in. If we assume our purchase and sales agreement for the deal will be $120,000, it means I am requesting $2,000 in an earnest money deposit. I will say it's non-refundable because the purchase and sales agreement between myself and the end buyer states that the contract is being bought in as-is condition.

So, if an inspection comes back bad, or an appraisal is low, that's tough. I'm selling the property in as-is condition, and the end buyer knew that. Either way, I'm getting my $2,000 as a non-refundable deposit. When I receive that money, I put it in an escrow account for the title company or attorney. At that point, I have my seller contact them to verify the funds have been deposited, and if they are requesting the funds to be dispersed for the earnest money deposit, the money can be dispersed at that time. This provides a little bit of insurance because if for some reason the transaction falls apart, the seller keeps that $1,000 and I keep the $1,000 remaining in the escrow account from my end buyer. Most of the time we aren't going to back out, but we can't guarantee that a complication won't arise with the end buyer.

You can always give someone else a limited power of attorney to allow them to sign on your behalf for the A to B, B to C transaction, too. This way, if you're out of the country, or if you're just too busy, maybe you have a job, and you can't get to the closing, for example, you could give a close friend, relative, realtor, or an attorney the capability of signing for you. When you assign limited power of attorney, you can close transactions from anywhere in the country. Normally, the limited power of attorney will come from the title company or the attorney, and they will prepare the document for you. Typically, there is a fee for this, and you will see it on the HUD closing statement.

Probate Review

There are massive benefits to getting involved with probate transactions. This is a quiet little niche whose success hinges on processing probates the right way and contacting the executors at the right time. As discussed, one of the best routes of finding probates and executors is to use attorneys, and outside of that tactic, to send a direct mail campaign.

You can also go through the public recorder, as we covered. Get involved in finding the right types of leads before anybody else does, and before anyone else reaches out to them. You can connect with these individuals very easily, and remember, you will also have an edge because not everyone is going to go after probates, either. If you're in a non-disclosure state like Indiana, it's tough to go out and buy lists of probates, because you will receive limited information. So, it's crucial that you develop relationships with attorneys. You can obtain the individual information needed to go to the county clerk's office to gather the rest of the information you must have to proceed.

When you deal in probates, you're going a step above and beyond what most people do when they get into flipping, especially if you're in a non-disclosure state.

If you don't know if you live in a non-disclosure state, just do a simple Google search. If this distinction applies to your state, it will be a little tougher to find the right types of individuals to contact. That said, it also opens you up to a huge advantage and opportunity because you will have the tools to get the right information; you will be able to step in front of anybody else. You won't likely close 8-12 probates every single month, but you can expect to get anywhere between one, two, and all the way up to five and six probates done. That's just in one particular market. If you want to deal in several markets, the sky's the limit.

You will have the ability to do this repeatedly because probate deals spring up constantly. Unfortunately, people do pass away, and most of the time the people who are left these properties are caught unaware of what to do. They may talk to a random attorney they don't know, maybe mom or dad structured something in a way where the heirs have no clue how to work with their requests. It could be overwhelming, and for you to come in as a real estate investor and help these folks out, it will just give them a more peaceful way to deal with the recent death and their hardship. You will set yourself apart because you will process the information you need, and you can reach out to these people in a way most investors can't.

Many investors send off a cheesy letter, telling people their sympathies and that they're sorry for the family's loss. First, you don't even know the person. Yes, you're trying to be nice, but most people can read right through that message. When you're upfront and honest with the contact about why you're reaching out to them, you will make far more progress in this manner.

The best thing I can leave you with is not to ever sell people on benefits. This is the worst and most inaccurate way to do business. Sell people on solutions. Listen to them. Eighty percent of sales made under contract will transpire because people listened. So, shut your mouth; listen to the owner of record and all the parties involved, and you will get the feedback you need to solve their problems. Your approach should center on resolving individuals' problems. Let people know you are the person who can do that for them. You're a solution maker. Once you realize you are a solution maker, you are going to get many more deals under contract simply by listening to other people.

Most of the time, if you just listen, you will understand the majority of people don't want the property. They have other heirs in the estate they must satisfy, but if you listen to them, you'll hear their emotions and wishes. Everybody's not one and the same; we all have different ways of dealing with death, and what we think will be the easiest path possible to manage it. I can tell you from experience; it's much easier dealing with somebody who understands what you're going through, and how to help you out in the best way possible than it is to hassle with people who don't listen and who have thinly-veiled motives.

Chapter 16: Get Ready to Flip

"The only thing standing in your way is you. Get out of your own way and make it happen. The time is right now right this second. You have the power to be and do anything you want in this life." - Jason Lucchesi

Back in 2008, when I began my career as a real estate investor, I really didn't have any direction on where to go. I got myself on a path going after shiny object after shiny object. I would attend different training webinars and buy different training programs that totaled about $40,000 to $45,000 in cash I didn't have. I was putting myself in a spot to where I was overwhelming myself with too much information.

I remember sitting on the floor in my office, having about $5 left to my name, living on unemployment check to unemployment check because I'd just left the mortgage industry, which, as most of you know, when the 2008 collapse happened, there wasn't anything left for loan officers. I had a small little sliver, but I was just starting my family, my son was on the way, and I was trying to get into real estate. It was completely overwhelmed with how much information there was. I was looking at apartments. I was looking at land. I was looking at rehabs. I was looking at all sorts of marketing strategies. I had so much on my plate; I didn't even know where to begin.

That brings me to this part in the book to where I want to tell you, you don't need to work in every single niche, in every single strategy taught here. I'm giving you permission right now to figure out which strategy you feel is going to be easiest for you, your schedule, and your outside life. Because you need balance. That was one of the things I didn't have. I'm encouraging you and letting you know right now you need to have balance, or else this endeavor isn't going to turn into a business that's going to make you happy and fulfilled. You need to go at this as a business, not a hobby. But you need to have the balance.

I would encourage you to pick anywhere between one, two, or three strategies from this book and implement them. Whenever I'm working with a client and they come in, I always recommend putting together a business plan. The business plan is the most important piece of your business. I'm not talking about drafting some long, drawn-out agenda. I'm talking about spending maybe two or three hours assembling a plan and listing out the three different action items you need to do.

Here's an example. Say you want to ignite your business. How are you going to do that? You need to know which direction you're going. Maybe your first item on your business plan is to find cash buyers. That's a goal. Find 15 cash buyers that are ready, willing, and able to pull the trigger when you send them deals. Cash buyers need to come first, especially if you're going to wholesale. If you're going to rehab, your cash buyers could also be private money lenders. If your business is in a more intermediate stage, then you can build on your existing circle. Advanced business owners can add buyers and private money lenders continually. This is a tool that you never want to neglect, so it gets dull.

Next, put your action steps below your goal. Take an example out of the chapters you've already read. Go to LinkedIn and look for real estate investors. Connect with 10 to 15 individuals on a daily basis by personalized message. Do that every single day, Sunday through Saturday.

Do the same thing on Facebook. Keep it at 10 to 15 messages. Be specific where you're going to find people. Make sure you're finding people who can actually do business with you. If you are in Los Angeles, California and you dig up somebody in IT consulting in Anchorage, Alaska, that's not going to be a good fit. You have to know a little bit about the person, find out if they're even involved in real estate, see if they want to do stuff in your neck of the woods. If you present the opportunity of why they should do business in your neighborhood, then that's fine. But don't just send off information because Jason's telling me to do this, this, and this. I'm not telling you to do anything. I'm telling you to use up your time in the right capacity to find people who will create a mutual benefit. If you can do business together, and both of you will be happy with the outcome. It's a win-win.

Inconsistency isn't going to get you consistent results. If you're going to be on LinkedIn, if you're going to be on Facebook, you must do it every single day. Make posts daily. Remember I gave you a tip to help you with content. Go to brainyquote.com, find some quotes, put them out there every single day, and be consistent. You might not get a lot of attention from it on the first couple of posts, but as you stay consistent with it, people will think, *"oh, Jason, I see his name coming through my newsfeed all the time. I like what he's doing. I like his quotes. He's got motivational pictures, too. I really like this guy."* When you do this people see that you're active. Can you outsource this too to a virtual assistant? Yes. We recommend upwork.com, or you could use fiverr.com. Staying consistent is a huge key to your business success.

Don't get sidetracked. A lot of us get sidetracked. We see shiny objects and tend to get attracted to them. One of the main subjects drawing people's attention right now is Bitcoin. People absolutely love Bitcoin. I've seen new investors come in, gung-ho about being a real estate investor, then six months go by, and their fire fades, and all of a sudden, they start seeing this info about Bitcoin. I'm not saying anything's wrong with Bitcoin, but you need to get laser focused; you need to put on the blinders and set a clear path of where you're going. Because if you don't know, it's like going to the grocery store without a list. If you go to the grocery store without a list, you're going to spend three times the amount of time strolling the aisles than you would if you had a grocery list.

The same concept applies to planning vacations. People spend hours more, if not days or weeks more, organizing a seven-day trip than they do on planning their life. When I say putting together a business plan, I'm talking about a one-page sheet. A six, seven or eight-page document is analysis paralysis. All that's going to do is send you off to read books, sign up for training programs and watch online seminars. Don't get me wrong, I still go to seminars. I still get coaching for life, for business, for anything I need. Once a successful person has crafted their way up to a certain position in life, they want to increase specific strengths, and so they hire coaches. There's nothing wrong with having a coach or going to seminars. We still need to make daily improvements, but you need to get laser focused in the beginning. Cut off the shiny object syndrome. Stop attending webinars that pitch you training programs.

You have to make time for action planning. It's great to read. You're taking action to increase your mind and make yourself smarter, to acquire more knowledge. But if you don't do anything with that knowledge, it becomes useless. Make sure you know exactly where you need to go, and you will see the success you ultimately want and desire by focusing on one to three strategies from this book.

We do have an online training you can attend. It will be more of a deep dive than the chapters you've read in this book. If you would like to attend, go to GetMyFlippingTraining.com. It's free. A 100 percent masterclass for you. But again, if you feel like it's going to be a distraction from this book and what you've read, I would encourage you to take the path you feel will be the easiest path, so you won't get so distracted.

I've been in a lot of positions as a real estate investor, and it does get easier when you can just concentrate on a couple of things at a time. If you feel like you need cash to give your business a jump-start, you're absolutely incorrect. I was on unemployment check to unemployment check. I barely had any money in my savings account. The first deal that I did brought in a little above $26,000. I still have a copy of that check as a reminder that when you set forth on a path you can make it happen. I didn't do my first deal until about eight months after I got started, and it was because I kept buying a bunch of training programs. I would get so excited when these programs came to the house, and they were wrapped in cellophane. I was so stoked! Then I opened them up and saw how much stuff was in the package. I thought, *where do I even begin? This is outrageous.*

Don't get overwhelmed. The path to success is to take massive, determined action. You have to do it. You have to take the action. A quote from Michael Jordan, who I absolutely love, since I'm originally from the Chicagoland area, is, "I can accept failure. Everyone fails at something. But I can't accept not trying." You have to try. And as you do, we're here for you. You can go to GetMyFlippingTraining.com. You can shoot us an email, at support@jasonlucchesi.com. Or you can give us a call at 317-900-1307. We would love to hear your success. We would love to hear how this book has transformed the way you do business. We would love to hear that you just recently closed a deal from one of the strategies taught here.

We sunk a ton of time into this book to guarantee you know we're not putting fluff out. We're putting action items in this book that we're using right now, today, and we're enjoying groundbreaking results. It's not because our team is superior. These teachings can be duplicated in your own business. We've helped thousands of students across the country, and they all absolutely love what we're doing. I know you will, too.

Let me tell you, if a kid like myself who barely graduated high school and who was told I wasn't going to graduate, who was voted "Least Likely to Succeed," can go from broke to six figures, to broke, to six figures, broke, and then to ultimately where I am now, I know for a fact you can do it. All you need is drive. I've been hit. I've been knocked down so many times that when I look back, it's almost surprising that I got back up. Some people stay down.

People get into a mediocre mindset and feel they need to do the nine-to-five grind Monday through Friday; then they enjoy their Saturday and Sunday, and dread going back to work on Monday. Get out of that mindset. You can enjoy every single day of the week. You don't have to dread Mondays. I absolutely love Mondays. Everybody on my team loves Mondays. You can make the money you want. You can create the lifestyle you want. You can have financial freedom. You can do what you want to do. Just set forth and take action. Don't ask me *what I take* to make my life happen. Ask me *what it takes*. You'll see the results you want if you go out and create them. As you go, remember we are here for you and in your corner.

Acknowledgments

Mats and Hil, the publishing dream team. Thank you for making my experience seamless, and a blast! My second book was just as much fun to write as the first. Now, to plan the third!

Resources

1. Zillow and Trulia
2. Rentometer.com
3. Sendspace.com
4. Dropbox.com
5. Google Drive
6. Google Voice
7. Hootsuite
8. Boostgram
9. Socialoomph.com
10. Mailchimp.com
11. Postlets.com
12. Cheapsigns.com
13. Docusign.com
14. Scheduleonce.com
15. Enounce.com
16. Zoom.us
17. GoToMeeting
18. Teamwork.com
19. Slack
20. Fiverr
21. HUDhomestore.com
22. Hubzu.com

23. Auction.com

24. Upwork.com

25. Callloop.com

26. Slybroadcast.com

27. Besttransactionfunding.com

28. Realtytrac.com

29. Craigslist.com

30. Tlo.com

31. IndianaVirtualLaw.com

32. MyINREIA.com

33. Prosperworks

34. Google Suite (G Suite)

About the Author

Jason Lucchesi founded the real estate investing company, Global Fortune Solutions in 2008 after finding quick success in the real estate industry. In 2002, he worked as a loan officer, then joined the nation's #1 lending institution, where he rapidly rose through the ranks to reach the #1 position in the country. After resigning his role, Jason pursued his dream of full-time entrepreneurship through Global Fortune Solutions. To date, Jason has partnered on over $225M in closed real estate transactions. Jason's expertise includes:

- Real estate coaching and mentoring
- Working directly with hedge funds, banks, private equity firms and private sellers

- Pre-foreclosures and foreclosures, HUD and government foreclosures, short sales, REOs
- Non-performing and performing notes
- Bulk packages: notes, residential and commercial properties
- Wholesaling residential and commercial properties
- Rehabs
- Apartment buildings
- Income producing properties
- Lease options
- Self-storage facilities

Jason has been married to his wonderful wife, Jamie, for 10 years, and they are the proud parents of three children: Brady (9), Gavin (7), and Cordelia (3).

49756119R00126

Made in the USA
Middletown, DE
23 June 2019